BY WAY OF GRACE

Moving from Faithfulness to Holiness

BY WAY OF GRACE

OF GRACE

Moving from Faithfulness to Holiness

PAULA HUSTON

LOYOLAPRESS.
CHICAGO

LOYOLAPRESS.
3441 N. ASHLAND AVENUE
CHICAGO, ILLINOIS 60657
(800) 621-1008
WWW.LOYOLABOOKS.ORG

Cover photograph: joSon/The Image Bank/Getty Images
Jacket and interior design: Loyola Press

Library of Congress Cataloging-in-Publication Data
Huston, Paula.
  By way of grace : moving from faithfulness to holiness / Paula Huston.
    p. cm.
  Includes bibliographical references.
  ISBN-13: 978-0-8294-2331-0
  ISBN-10: 0-8294-2331-1
  1. Christian life. 2. Virtues. 3. Prayer—Christianity. I. Title.
  BV4501.3.H88 2007
  241'.4—dc22
                          2006033675

Printed in the United States of America
07 08 09 10 11 12 Bang 10 9 8 7 6 5 4 3 2 1

For my teachers, with love and gratitude

CONTENTS

INTRODUCTION ix

1 Prudence, the Art of Seeing Clearly 1

2 Temperance, the Art of Holding a Balance 21

3 Fortitude, the Art of Courageous Continuing 37

4 Justice, the Art of Forgiving 55

5 Humility, the Art of Honest Self-Appraisal 75

6 Faith, the Art of Believing in Things Unseen 103

7 Hope, the Art of Patient Waiting 127

8 Charity, the Art of Loving the Enemy 153

EPILOGUE 181

NOTES 185

BIBLIOGRAPHY 199

INTRODUCTION

For just as ascetic practice gives birth to virtue,
so contemplation engenders spiritual knowledge.
St. Maximus the Confessor (c. 580–662)[1]

High in the Rockies and sliced through by cold, copper-green
streams, the Colorado Plateau spoke to me the moment we came
over the rise and coasted down into its lonely expanse of marsh
grass and fluttering aspens. The vast alpine plain, rimmed with jut-
ting bare peaks, looked like Arctic tundra. Somewhere far above
us a red-tailed hawk wheeled through the endless blue sky; I could
hear its long waterfall of a scream above the hum of the engine, and
for a moment the sound cracked my heart wide open. *This is it,* I
thought, with a joyful uprush of suppressed longing. *Finally: a place
without people.*

The only trouble was that I was not here on retreat. Instead, my
husband, Mike, and I were heading for an isolated group of cabins clustered at the bank of the Tarryall River, where we were to
meet up with my many siblings and their families. There we would
spend the next five days having a high old time: drinking wine, toss-
ing the Frisbee, barbecuing, hiking, playing never-ending games of
Scrabble, and dredging up childhood memories. Stunned at the
irony—I'd finally found the perfect solitary hideout, only to have
it colonized for family partying—I slumped against the back of the
seat. It wasn't that I didn't love my sibs, their spouses, or their kids.
I loved them a lot, which made my problem even more baffling.

This urge to flee human contact, even with people I adored as much as I did my extended clan, had been putting a damper on all my relationships for the past several years. It had first manifested itself when I began visiting a Camaldolese Benedictine monastery on the California Big Sur coast, a community of hermit-monks who lived on the side of a mountain high above the Pacific. Amazing things had happened to me there: a return to the Christianity I had long since abandoned; a conversion to Catholicism; a powerful new desire to learn how to pray; the discovery of an ancient tradition I'd never heard about in the Sunday schools of my youth.

I couldn't get enough of all this and disappeared as often as I could into the silence and solitude of the Big Sur hermitage. Naturally, my new passion for religious retreats had an effect on family and friends. Some of them—Mike, for example—found the whole enterprise dubious and disconcerting. What was happening to his formerly sociable wife? Why was I so moody and withdrawn these days? When had I become such a sensitive plant?

I imagine it was hard to take me seriously, though the people who loved me (including the very sibs with whom we were about to rendezvous) certainly tried to be understanding. "You've been working too hard for years," they assured me, "and you *should* take more vacations." The word *vacation*, however, set my teeth on edge. What did they think I was doing up there with the monks—water-skiing? Others pointed to my flock of four young adults barely out of their teens and shook their heads knowingly. "No wonder you can hardly wait to get away. Don't blame you a bit." It's not that, I wanted to protest. It's not that I'm simply tired or burned out. It's . . . *bigger* than that.

I couldn't be more specific, for I hardly understood it myself, this late-blooming love affair with God that had so totally shifted the focus and direction of my life. Nor had I yet figured out how to deal with the difficult new personality that had invaded my old familiar self. I was embarrassed at the brooding, sardonic, Heathcliff-like person I'd become but had no idea what to do about it. The world seemed too much with me; I felt as though I were living without skin, and every sound (TV, radio, dial-up modems), every sensation (students jostling me as I crisscrossed campus each day), and every image (bumper stickers, T-shirts emblazoned with profound thoughts, scantily clad bodies on billboards) had become an assault on the senses.

I couldn't avoid the suspicion that this painful state was linked to my hermitage visits. Somehow, the extended time alone on retreat, the hours of silent sitting on benches overlooking the sea, the predawn chanting of psalms during Vigil seemed to have wreaked havoc with my normal capacity to handle stimuli. I worried about this. After all, I was not a monk and never would be. My home was in the world, not in the monastery.

Meanwhile, we had arrived at the Tarryall River and were pulling onto the gravel driveway that led to the cabins. I could feel myself tensing for the inevitable onslaught. For a sweet, blessed moment, all was silence and green pines; then out came my sisters, waving and hollering, and there went my brother's dog, Breeze, ripping past after a rabbit, and here came three of my giggling, already-sunburned nieces. The reunion had begun: food, hooting laughter, family photo sessions, the garrulous camaraderie of folks who love but rarely get to see one another.

For me, however, the fun was shadowed by a sense of being dangerously overwhelmed. Later, photo after photo would reveal just how aggrieved I had been. I spent much of the time hiding in our cabin, telling everyone I had a writing deadline to meet. When my sibs tried to lure me out with sport, I made transparent excuses. I snapped at one of my brothers-in-law (a merciless tease), then skulked around in a dither of guilt and irritation. And when our reunion was finally over, I confessed to the sister who had worked so hard to put it together, a sister who had driven nearly a thousand miles to be with us, that I wouldn't be up for another one anytime soon. Then, feeling fragile and misunderstood, I scheduled myself for another hermitage retreat.

Fortunately, my inability to cope with the world eventually disappeared as mysteriously as it had arrived. First, however, I had to make some serious changes in the way I lived, many of them deliberately intended to create more opportunities for solitude and silence. Though some of these shifts—giving up my teaching career, for example—were not easy, I found that when I stopped fighting this strange urge to be alone, time and space opened up. Broken relationships—those that had survived—slowly began to heal. I stopped feeling like a person at war with herself.

Over the next few years, I read, I talked with the monks, and I wrote in my journal, trying to piece together just what had happened to me. Though I toyed with a number of theories—the onset of menopause, or one of Gail Sheehy's innumerable adult "passages," or a straight-ahead nervous breakdown—deep down I suspected I'd been through some kind of important spiritual transition. But what? And why me?

Then one day I read a verse I'd read a hundred times before. In it Christ says, "Let anyone who thirsts come to me and drink. Whoever believes in me, as scripture says: 'Rivers of living water will flow from within him'" (John 7:37–38, NAB). Suddenly these words were striking home in a whole new way. For it was certainly true that ever since my prodigal-daughter return to Christianity and those first trips to the hermitage, I'd felt a nearly unbearable spiritual thirst. However, it had not before occurred to me that this thirsty time might finally pass, that streams of living water could begin to flow from within *me*. How could this be?

I found my answer in a slender classic called *Teach Us to Pray*. Here Trappist monk and scholar André Louf discusses the plight of modern Christians in regard to what he considers to be a basic fact of life. He says that the contemporary Western world has lost its connection with prayer. In the old days when prayer was taken for granted, the temptation may have been for people to believe they were praying when instead they were simply talking to themselves. But now, he thinks, we are experiencing the opposite extreme; now "we have lost the scent of prayer altogether."[2] And without prayer, we are in danger of perishing of spiritual thirst, no matter how firmly we hold our beliefs.

How do we recover our connection with prayer? According to Louf, we must first find and listen to our heart, though not in the contemporary sense of paying attention to our feelings. Instead, we are to seek the *biblical* heart, that "organ of prayer" within us that is designed to be in continual contact with God. When we finally come upon it, we discover something truly amazing: our heart, like an intricate clock set into motion at baptism, is already praying on its own. However, unless we reduce the clamor around us and quiet down ourselves, it is nearly impossible to hear it.

Hence, the need for silence, which is so difficult to find in our noisy, hyperactive society. Anybody who seriously seeks it out is bound to feel guilty and misanthropic for a while, just as I did. To incorporate periods of silence into our lives requires major changes, some of them painful. Certainly, our most important relationships are shaken, as were mine.

But unless we quiet down enough to pick up the sound of our praying heart, we continue to thirst. And as long as we remain unaware of our secretly praying heart, we fail to see the light in which we live and therefore cannot grasp the supernatural side of our identity as human beings. Without knowing who we are, we cannot fathom who we are meant to be. We remain faithful but untransformed, and without such transformation we can never become a source of living water for others.

Thus, this first astonished glimpse of the secretly praying heart is only the beginning of a long journey. To stay the course we must continue to grow and develop spiritually. The hazy outlines of the "new man" in Christ must become more and more sharply defined against the dark backdrop of the world. For we are not being called out of this world after all, but marshaled into God's earthly service. Our daily activities, mundane as they may seem, are meant to reflect the light of Christ to other people. We are being prepared for a life we can hardly imagine, and for real transformation to take place we must actively participate in the process.

Without knowing who we are, we cannot fathom who we are meant to be. We remain faithful but untransformed.

As Paul puts it, we must "work out [our] salvation with fear and trembling" (Philippians 2:12). God provides us with the power of his grace, but focused, strenuous human effort is also required to coax out the person we are meant to be. "Clothe yourselves with compassion, kindness, humility, gentleness and patience," Paul says. "Bear with each other and forgive whatever grievances you may have against one another. Forgive as the Lord forgave you" (Colossians 3:12–13). Clearly, the path we are now on requires that we develop spiritual strength. Christians have long turned to a particular method—the practice of the virtues—as an aid to their own metamorphosis.

By Way of Grace is about this spiritual transformation that Christ's life, death, and resurrection makes possible for human beings. It focuses on two key aspects of the Christian transformative process: listening ever more deeply to the organ of prayer as it communes with God (contemplation) and cooperating with grace to develop spiritual strength (the practice of the virtues).

Since we naturally turn to human exemplars when we are try-ing to grasp something new, each chapter in this book is devoted to a great contemplative saint. Beginning with the early centu-ries of the church (Basil of Caesarea, Gregory the Great), and moving on to medieval times (Bernard of Clairvaux, Thomas Aquinas), the Renaissance (Teresa of Ávila, Francis de Sales), and the modern era (Thérèse of Lisieux, Edith Stein), *By Way of Grace* traces out the ageless and universal pattern of Christian transformation. Out of the eight saints featured in the book, seven are doctors of the church, which means that their writ-ings have in some special way contributed to the evolution of Catholic doctrine.

In addition, at the heart of every chapter sits one of the tradi-tional Christian virtues, those habitual strengths that St. Thomas Aquinas says are developed through repeated good acts within the structure of our daily lives. The cardinal virtues of prudence, tem-perance, fortitude, and justice, once so beloved by the politically astute Greeks and soldierly Romans, are made new by the contemplative framework of Christianity. Transformed in purpose by the incarnation event, the cardinal virtues are what help us put on the new

> *I learned that the sudden, inexplicable disruption of my comfortable life was something to be welcomed rather than feared.*

person in Christ. They in turn are strengthened by the great theo-logical virtues of faith, hope, and love, gifts of grace bequeathed at baptism. All are tempered by the monastic virtue of humility, the childlike clarity that opens the doors of the kingdom.

Finally, *By Way of Grace* intertwines the wisdom of the saints and the power of the virtues with the story of my own spiritual struggles. For the sake of my beleaguered siblings at that family reunion on the Colorado Plateau, it is certainly time to sort it all out. Even more important, however, is the fact that in these secular times, spiritual eyewitnesses are needed. I wish I had known ahead of time, for example, that the sudden, inexplicable disruption of my comfortable life was something to be welcomed rather than feared. I wish I had known that this temporary shattering of all that is loved and familiar is a critical phase of the spiritual journey.

For it is only when we surrender to the mysterious work of the Holy Spirit within us that we ourselves become oases in the midst of a contemporary spiritual wasteland. As a long-ago Byzantine monk once put it, "Looking back, my impression is that for many, many years I was carrying prayer within my heart, but did not know it at the time. It was like a spring, but one covered by a stone. Then at a certain moment Jesus took the stone away. At that the spring began to flow and has been flowing ever since."

> *I wish I had known that this temporary shattering of all that is loved and familiar is a critical phase of the spiritual journey.*

These, I believe, are the living waters that Christ promised. They bear on their tide our new self, "renewed in knowledge in the image of its creator." They carry us on their crest to places we cannot imagine. And most important of all, they allow us to share in that divine love that alone can slake the world's terrible thirst.

1
PRUDENCE
THE ART OF SEEING CLEARLY

Prudence springs from contemplation in the
sphere of things good and evil.
St. Basil of Caesarea (c. 330–79)[1]

I had been thrashing about for hours, and by the soft, disjointed snorts coming out of Mike, I could hear that he was barely hanging on to the edges of whatever dream he was trying to have. Poor man. This was my third night of insomnia in a row—a record even for me, the nocturnal happy wanderer—and the worst part was that nothing was yet resolved.

I knew that when I woke up the next morning, *if* I finally got to sleep in time to require an actual waking, I would be fifty years old. And somehow I'd gotten it firmly in mind that a decision I'd been postponing for several years, the decision about whether to continue on with my university teaching job or to take a shamefully early retirement, had to be made by my fiftieth birthday.

Why? No real reason, except that on my fiftieth birthday I would become eligible to receive a pension from the system, not to mention a packet of medical benefits that, given the current lunatic cost of insurance, was worth several of my weights in gold. This decision, which could obviously be put off indefinitely if I so chose, was for some reason pressing inexorably down upon me; I could hardly breathe because of the urgent need to *do something now* about the confused mass of *should*s and *ought*s and *wish I could*s that had been banging around inside me for so long.

If only I could think straight! If only I had a wise adviser! If only, if only . . . the irony being that I had talked myself blue in the face with anyone not in my department who would listen—Mike, colleagues at other universities, even my poor twentysomething kids, who could not quite grasp why their mom, gainfully employed in a career they could only wish for in this current job market, would consider leaving. "But you like teaching, don't you?" they asked, honestly confused.

"Of course—I love it," I said. "That's not the point."

"So the point is . . . ? Help us out here, Mom."

But this was the question I could not answer, despite the long months of strenuous mental debate. And now the self-imposed deadline loomed: fifty was rising with the dawn sun.

Sweating and desperate, I plunged my face into the pillow and moaned out loud, "Tell me what to do, God!" Within thirty seconds, words were coming right back at me, strong, clear, and unmistakable: *Surrender—just yield.*

Surrender? Give up the long bloody battle to wrestle this decision to the ground? Let it go, just like that?

All right, I thought. *I will.* And I promptly fell deeply asleep. Two hours later, as I stumbled out of bed to turn off the alarm, I realized that new words were hanging in the air: *You're done.* Since this was the clearest message I'd had in months of writing out priority lists, comparing financial scenarios, badgering people, recording long pros and cons in my journal, and praying for guidance, I decided to go with it. I sat down at the computer, typed up a resignation letter, made copies for my department head and dean, put them in envelopes, and headed off for campus. Within two months I was walking away from my last class at the university, twenty years of employment ended with a simple "You're done."

Needing to See

Had I made the right decision? Only time would tell. First I had to go through the inevitable second-guessing. Maybe, I thought, I'd really quit because of some self-centered urge I couldn't acknowledge, so I *pretended* God had spoken to me. Maybe teaching, which I'd always thought I loved so much, had been starting to drive me nuts on a subconscious level, and if it really was starting to drive me nuts, then maybe I should have continued on with it to find out what God was trying to teach me.

Maybe, on the other hand, I'd been called to leave because it had become too easy for me. I did it well, my ego was constantly reinforced by my students, and the classroom provided a built-in social arena I was going to miss. More, in teaching there was no room for malaise, ennui, the noonday devil; I had to maintain high-energy good spirits no matter what. Yet life had its somber sides, and I needed to face up to that.

And on and on and on.

Though the back-and-forth on this decision I had already made ended soon enough, it was followed by something more serious: a siege of spiritual darkness that went on for several years. Was this proof I'd chosen badly? Only after the black season ended did I finally understand: I needed to quit the job because it was getting in the way of yet another spiritual transition—a bleak, lonely, but necessary time that could be experienced only when the landscape had been cleared. In other words, I'd made the right choice.

But how, exactly? It didn't seem that I'd actually decided anything, only given up at the end out of sheer exhaustion. And I would be faced with such major decisions again, either my own or those confronting other people. I needed to learn a more reliable decision-making method than the emotionally tumultuous, sleep-deprived sorry excuse for one I'd used in the past. If God hadn't saved me from myself, I'd still be hammering my pillow in frustration each night.

I suspected that the method I was seeking might lie buried somewhere in the past, because I had discovered, with the guidance of the monks, other long-lost spiritual treasures in the books of a handful of contemporary Christian "archaeologists." These scholars had introduced me, for example, to the almost-abandoned spiritual disciplines of fasting, silence, solitude, and *lectio divina*, or holy reading. They'd pointed me toward the original Christian method of meditative prayer as recorded in the fifth-century *Institutes* and *Conferences* of St. John Cassian. They'd translated the *Praktikos* of Cassian's teacher, Evagrius Ponticus, along with his instructions about "watching the thoughts."

The Point of Prudence

I was pretty sure early Christianity had also come up with a way to make a good decision, and I even had an inkling of where I'd uncover the method: in the ancient cardinal virtues. Very early on—in fact, as soon as I began to read about prudence—I found what I was looking for. Indeed they'd had a method, an ingenious one at that, but the worldview on which it was based now seemed outmoded, even alien. Could it still work for contemporary people? That seemed doubtful.

"To the contemporary mind," says philosopher and Thomist scholar Josef Pieper, "prudence seems less a prerequisite to goodness than an evasion of it."[2] In other words, the word *prudence* has picked up negative connotations in our time. Pieper blames our present attitude toward prudence on an unconsciously held but deeply influential romantic worldview picked up early in the nineteenth century via the great British Romantic poets. Romanticism insists that the highest kind of life—in fact, the only life worth living—is one of constant striving for what can never be achieved. The true romantic doesn't care; he launches himself heedlessly into the universe and flames out when young. On the romantic trajectory, any stopping to assess can lead to stalling out, and so one never stops. Better to live by the passions, risk all, and die a hero.

Much of the aggressive hyperactivity of our culture is linked to this notion that passionate, spontaneous action is worth far more than considered thought. We've come to see unchecked impulsiveness—another key romantic value—as "natural" and thus good. Prudence, which demands clear vision, careful thought, and the temporary banking of the fires of emotion, is therefore deeply suspect for many contemporary people. Like the nineteenth-century romantics, we believe that only the passionate really live, that the happiest and richest life is the one lived with gusto, and that the prudent—those who ponder deeply before taking action—are really just cowards pretending to be wise.

We also suspect that prudent people may be self-deceptive. The legacy of another major nineteenth-century thinker, Freud, has greatly shaped our thinking about what we can and cannot know about ourselves. His theory of the unconscious has so permeated the contemporary Western worldview that we can no longer imagine clear and objective thinking to be possible. He taught us that so-called rational thought can act in a frighteningly devious way—as a reassuring screen between us and what's really going on at the deeper and more mysterious level of the unconscious mind.

Finally, from nineteenth-century Darwinian biology we inherit the notion that the world is a jungle, only the strong survive, and he who hesitates is lost. Under this view, it is far better to act swiftly and instinctively and sort it all out later, for waiting can prove fatal. If this is our reality—and many contemporary people, including Christians, believe it is—then gut reaction obviously serves us better than careful thought.

The very word itself—*prudence*—sounds crabbed, miserly, puckered. We see it as a trait of those who overvalue personal safety and comfort. The prudent, we think, are the sort of folks who stop to untie their shoes, fold their clothes, and lay their glasses carefully aside before attending to the drowning man hollering for help.

Yet for much of Christian history, prudence has been the primary cardinal virtue. For the ancients, prudence referred to the "perfected ability to make right decisions."[3] It had to be present in order for the other three cardinal virtues of temperance, justice, and fortitude to qualify as virtues at all. Prudence in this original sense describes a kind of spiritual vision, the capacity to see and comprehend the nature of reality.

Prudence describes a kind of spiritual vision, the capacity to see and comprehend the nature of reality.

This clarity of vision allows prudent people to discern the truth of a situation and to recognize what particular action they must take that will lead to the good. Then it enables them to follow through.

People can act bravely, justly, or well without prudence, but practicing the virtue of prudence means that all our actions are rooted in this clear vision of reality. When we act without prudence, our motives are unclear: maybe, for example, we are simply pretending to be brave or secretly showing off our intelligence or even doing the right thing through lucky accident. We cannot be relied upon to react the same way the next time around; we may be swayed by a different emotion, for example, or by a recent new idea. On the other hand, if we try to establish a basis for our decisions by operating solely from principle, we also act imprudently, for no rule can possibly cover all the complexities of human relationships. Though some of us—those we think of as "naturally good"—may instinctively lean in the right direction much of the time, this instinct remains a bare uncertain urge, not the "perfected ability" of prudence.

There was a beautiful simplicity and lightness to the practice of prudence that appealed to me. But I could see two big impediments to it in our contemporary world. Not only do we have trouble believing that it is even possible to see the true nature of reality, but we also can no longer agree on what it is we are looking at.

The twentieth century was tough on us in this regard. Freudian psychoanalytic thought permeated modern literature and gave us a picture of our mental selves as divided into two realms: the thin, sunny strip of light we call the conscious mind and the immense, murky, impenetrable abyss of the unconscious that lies below it, burbling away on its own like a Yellowstone mud pot. The notion that our weakling conscious mind can even begin to see clearly under these circumstances seems misguided, even absurd. How can we trust our vision when dark unconscious forces are so insidiously at work in us? Aren't we simply kidding ourselves, projecting our wishes on the world and then believing in the illusion?

The belief that it is impossible to see objectively forms the basis of much contemporary thought: pluralism, which insists that cultures are self-contained worlds, impenetrable by outsiders; relativism, which denies the possibility of absolute truth and claims instead that all "truths" are subjective and individual; emotivism, which theorizes that morality is not about good and evil but what we personally like or abhor. Through the earnest efforts of social reformers from the sixties on, we have become skittish about passing judgments on *anything*, including our own ability to see and think clearly.

To make things even tougher, we're still dealing with the ramifications of nineteenth-century biology under their many guises in modern literature, economic theory, behavioral psychology, and philosophy. This view, perhaps most bleakly portrayed by the great naturalist writers of the early twentieth century, holds that life is brutal and short and ends in death and decay. More, the forces of nature are both inexorable and uncaring: they grind up whole mountain ranges, given enough time. Humans are simply intelligent animals with a particular slot on the food chain, genetically determined creatures with no hope of transcending the hand they were dealt at birth. Life has no inherent meaning; it is up to the individual person to create, however ineptly, his own reason to go on. With such a heavy legacy weighing us down, it's almost impossible to think in terms of "spiritual vision" and "the nature of reality."

I realized that for prudence to become a modern virtue, we need first of all to resurrect the Christian cosmos in all its glory— that vision of an extravagantly beautiful universe resting in the hands of its loving and deeply involved Creator, who cares even about the deaths of sparrows. Then we have to trust that God would not have invited us into his divine life unless he gave us the ability to see where we were going. We can't look for something we don't entirely believe is there, and even if we do believe it, we won't seek it if we think our eyes are defective. We have to know before we begin that the kingdom of heaven, with all its assurances about the deaf now hearing and the blind now seeing, is indeed among us.

To do this in contemporary times, however, we need to reconnect with those who knew the Christian cosmos as though it were home. And what people, I thought, were more familiar with this marvelous landscape than the mighty spiritual warriors of the third and fourth centuries? If anyone needed the virtue of prudence, it was these early definers of Christianity, working out their still-infant religion right at the crossroads of East and West.

> *If anyone needed the virtue of prudence, it was these early definers of Christianity, working out their still-infant religion right at the crossroads of East and West.*

St. Basil: Who Brought Moderation to Monastic Life

Off I went to the library to see what I could discover about one of the most influential early Christians, St. Basil of Caesarea, or Basil the Great. I knew he had written a lot about contemplation, and given his amazingly productive life, I was guessing he'd also had some salient things to say about prudence. Perhaps he was the man who could teach me how to make a decision.

Basil was born in Cappadocia, present-day Turkey, around the year 330. His family was one of the most remarkable of his day: his devoutly Christian parents, Basil and Emmelia, produced nine children, three of whom became saints. Among the siblings were three bishops, a hermit, and a nun. Basil's grandmother Macrina the Elder helped set the standard for the family: a fugitive during the persecutions of Christians under the emperors Diocletian and Maximian, she was also a well-known disciple of St. Gregory Thaumaturgus.[4]

Basil gave his grandmother credit for his earliest spiritual training, calling her "the distinguished Macrina" and declaring that she had carefully retained the wise sayings of her holy mentor and used these in the "education and formation of the tiny child I was at the time." It was she who brought him up in the "doctrines of piety."[5]

However, it was another Macrina, Basil's older sister and fellow saint, who ushered him to the threshold of his vocation. Gifted and intelligent, he'd gone off to study first in Caesarea, then Constantinople, then Athens, seemingly destined to follow in his father's footsteps as a rhetorician. While living in Athens he met the friend of his life, fellow student Gregory of Nazianzus, who was also to become a saint and a doctor of the church. The two of them talked early on about Basil's secret dream: a hermitage in the forest where they could live in solitude and silence, devoting themselves to prayer.

When Basil graduated from his studies and returned to the family estate at Annesi, he was a brilliant twenty-five-year-old, qualified to teach rhetoric and philosophy. He was immediately offered a job in Neocaesarea and went to work on what would clearly become a highly successful career. Macrina the Younger, however, knew his heart and knew that he was becoming increasingly drawn to the kind of monastic life then unfolding in the Egyptian desert.

She saw that he was fascinated by the hundreds of men and women who were flocking away from the big intellectual centers of Alexandria and Rome and heading out to the wilderness. She recognized and understood his yearning to visit the holy men and women in their desert caves or the monks of the gigantic monasteries founded by St. Pachomius. Macrina urged Basil to follow these spiritual promptings, advising him to renounce his career, undergo baptism, and dedicate his life totally to God.

Shortly thereafter, he underwent a dramatic conversion experience. "One day, arising as from a deep sleep I looked out upon the marvelous light of the truth of the Gospel, and beheld the uselessness of the wisdom 'of the princes of this world that come to naught.'"[6] Seeing that all he had studied and learned amounted to nothing in light of how badly his character had been "perverted by association with the wicked," he went to the words of Christ for guidance.[7] There he found the same radical call to arms that has prompted saints throughout the centuries to relinquish social status and give away all that they have to the poor.

Newly baptized, Basil headed to Egypt in search of a guide. Among the hermitages and monasteries of the desert, he became an important eyewitness to one of the more amazing spiritual experiments in history. His yearlong travels took him eventually to Palestine, Syria, and Mesopotamia, where the same phenomenon was occurring. Of the desert dwellers he visited, he said, "I marveled at their steadfastness in sufferings, I was amazed at their vigour in prayers, at how they gained mastery over sleep, being bowed down by no necessity of nature, ever preserving exalted and unshackled the purpose of their soul, in hunger and thirst, in cold and nakedness, not concerning themselves with the body, nor deigning to waste a thought upon it." He called them sojourners on earth with "citizenship in heaven" and prayed to become their "emulator."[8]

Back home from his travels, he founded a small Christian commune in Annesi on the banks of the Iris. He was ordained as a hieromonk (priest) by Eusebius of Caesarea, and in 370 he succeeded Eusebius as bishop of the first see of Cappadocia.[9] First, however, he spent years developing a model for monastic life, incorporating what he had learned in the desert. He was convinced by his travels that the Pachomian monasteries, though far too large, were closer to the gospel ideal than was the completely solitary hermit existence.

For one thing, it was dangerous to enter this portion of the spiritual path alone, and Basil warned that "they who are set apart from ordinary life in the world and follow a regimen more nearly approaching the divine life should not undertake this discipline of their own accord or as solitaries."[10] In addition, he believed that

Christian virtues could not be lived out except in community. As he put it in the Long Rules, which were his instructions to the communities he founded, "The doctrine of the charity of Christ does not permit the individual to be concerned solely with his own private interests."[11] Finally, the goal of monastic life was sanctity, and a group living by a common rule could require accountability from its members: "It is fitting that such a way of life have a witness, that it may be free of base suspicion."[12]

Basil recommended moderate-sized separate monasteries for men and women of all classes ("Members of the female sex are not rejected because of physical weakness, but, chosen for the army of Christ by reason of their virility of spirit").[13] These communities, devoted to manual labor and daily prayer, were to share sleeping quarters and meals.[14]

Basil's model became the prototype for Western monasticism as we see it developed later in the Rule of St. Benedict. The hallmark of the Basilian monastery was moderation, which meant reasonable limitations for ascetic practices such as fasting and vigils. Basil was convinced that extreme self-deprivation could lead to a deadly pride and that idealistic young monks would progress faster by obeying an experienced superior who could keep careful watch over them.[15] The use of material items such as clothing and food was to be regulated by need rather than desire or strict rules: "Wine, also, should not be held in abomination if it is taken for curative purposes and is not craved beyond necessity."[16]

A true monastic community, Basil believed, offered the best venue for life based on the "double commandment of love."[17] Basil saw Matthew 22:37–39 as foundational. In this passage, Christ responds to the question of the Pharisee—"Teacher, which is the greatest commandment in the Law?"—with a two-part answer: "'Love the Lord your God with all your heart and with all your soul

and with all your mind.' This is the first and greatest commandment. And the second is like it: 'Love your neighbor as yourself.'"
Basil understood the first as calling for separation from the world,
and the second for community rooted in and nourished by *caritas*,
or true *koinonia*, a beautiful term used in early monastic communities for the loving sharing of goods and a common rule for life.[18]

Partaking of Divine Nature

What was the hoped-for result? "Man, according to St. Basil, is a
creature who has received a commandment to become God," explains
Orthodox theologian Vladimir Lossky.[19] Basil and the other Eastern
fathers of the church believed that Christians are people undergoing
transformation—deification—through obedience to the commandments and the promptings of the Holy Spirit. This divinization of
humanity is in fact the primary purpose of Christ's incarnation. As
Basil's contemporary St. Athanasius put it, "For the Son of God
became man so that we might become God."[20]

The transformation process cannot begin, however, without
clear spiritual vision. We have to see who we are and what we are
meant to be before we can work together with God to achieve our
proper end. Basil said, "The eye that wanders continually around,
now sideways, now up and down, is unable to see distinctly what lies
under it; it ought rather to apply itself firmly to the visible object if
it aims at a clear vision. Likewise, the spirit of man, if it is dragged
about by the world's thousand cares, has no way to attain a clear
vision of the truth."[21]

How do we free ourselves of the "thousand cares" in order to get
a clear line of sight? "There is only one escape: withdrawal from the
world altogether." Basil was very serious about this need to sever
the ties that bind, and he did not confine his advice to monks. He
believed that as Christians, we are all meant to free ourselves from

dependence on possessions, social identity, security systems, and the intellect, "making ready to receive in our heart the imprint of divine teaching."[22] As Christ so clearly stated, we must lose our life in order to find it.

But this is just the first step; the next requires the action of the Holy Spirit within us, which comes only when there is a real willingness to be transformed. That willingness is manifested by our ongoing attempt to live as virtuously as we can: with prudence, temperance, justice, fortitude, humility, faith, hope, and love. However, our "own positive efforts and activities are merely preparatory," says Benedictine oblate Cyril Karam, "to the higher activity of the Spirit present in us."[23] This higher activity is grace, in which a new capacity is released within our normal human powers.

The stage that follows, Basil tells us, is "like a sun taking hold of an eye which has been purified."[24] We are now true contemplatives, and the Holy Spirit is "able to divinize the 'temple' in which he dwells."[25] "By him hearts are lifted, the weak are led by the hand, the proficient become perfect. . . . From this comes foresight of the future, understanding of mysteries, comprehension of hidden things, distribution of charisms, heavenly citizenship, singing with the angelic choirs, joy without end, permanent abode in God, likeness to God, and finally the supremely desirable object: 'becoming God.'"[26]

Here, I could see, was the lost Christian cosmos in all its glory, a place where rivers of living water could indeed flow within mere human beings. At the core of this magnificent image of the universe was St. Basil's vision of human life and its ultimate purpose—to become God. I knew that Eastern Orthodoxy has not departed from this vision in seventeen hundred years, but Basil's influence seemed harder to locate in contemporary Catholicism and Protestantism. Were all Christians on the same page regarding the nature of reality? Did Christian contemplation mean the same thing to every denomination? Was Basil's version of prudence—seeing clearly, comprehending the truth of a situation, then determining the action that would lead to the good—workable even today?

It didn't take me long to verify that Catholicism still holds Basil's view. Though Catholics generally use the phrase *union with God* in place of the Orthodox term *deification*, each refers to the same goal: as the *Catechism* puts it, "The Word became flesh to make us *'partakers of the divine nature.'*"[27] St. John of the Cross describes this process thus: "What God seeks, he being himself God by nature, is to make us gods through participation, just as fire converts all things through fire."[28]

I soon realized that most Protestants also maintain this belief. Though they traditionally refer to the end point of the Christian transformation process as "glorification" rather than "union with God" or "deification," and though they believe it does not occur until after death, some Protestants describe the divine/human relationship much as Basil would. Anglican bishop Joseph Hall, for example, speaks of the Christian as one who "walks on earth, but converses in heaven: having his eyes fixed on the invisible, and enjoying a sweet communion with his God."[29]

What Prudence Is and Isn't

I could now look back with new eyes on those long, confusing, and emotional months of decision making that finally resulted in my early retirement. And I saw two things I hadn't seen before. First, there had been nothing much like prudence involved—a lot of passionate emoting, certainly, but little real vision. Second, under all the layers of *should*s and *ought*s and *wish I could*s had been something that—thanks be to God!—partook of the very nature of reality anyway, despite my complete inability to see it. Underneath everything else had been an already-praying heart, waiting to become a temple of the Holy Spirit. And it was this heart that had finally prevailed.

As my new life began to unfold, it became clearer and clearer that there had been no other option in my case than Basil's physical withdrawal from the world. Although at the time this had felt like pure flight, possibly escapist, I could now see otherwise. I hadn't been so much fleeing people or responsibility as wriggling free of a particular framework that no longer reflected my deepest commitments. Philosopher Charles Taylor uses the term *framework* to describe the set of mostly unquestioned beliefs that "define the demands" by which we judge our lives and measure their "fullness or emptiness."[30] A framework houses us and gives our lives whatever meaning we think they have.

As a Christian in the middle of a modern secular university campus, I had been trying to inhabit two different frameworks. Struggling to respond to the demands of both, I'd become trapped in a lonely and confusing no-man's-land. Though I genuinely longed for the "transfigured vision" of the saints, I was at the same time still firmly attached to modern academic values of self-assertiveness, competition, public recognition of achievement, and ranking based on merit. I saw now that I had quite a bit more letting go to do before I could safely return to a campus career—for perhaps God would call me back someday. But for the present, I was where I needed to be.

I looked at my new life and saw that even though I had more time for silence and solitude and now experienced on a daily basis what I'd once tried so desperately to get during those hermitage retreats, I was still deeply immersed in community. Besides our large family of twentysomething children and their significant others who continued to flow through the house on a regular basis, there were our many neighbors on the country road, some of them elderly, some of them lonely, some of them needing help.

There were also my myriad sibs—still loyal despite that ill-fated family reunion—and Mike's too, plus all the attendant nieces and nephews. There were our parents, now in their eighties, and old friends, and the large group of oblates connected with the hermit-age who lived in our area. And there were the strangers, the travel-ers, the pilgrims who had always wandered into and out of our lives and didn't stop now. I was having more spontaneous interactions with people as an officially retired person than I'd ever had as a teacher.

The need for prudence, that practical spiritual vision Basil calls "contemplation in the sphere of things good and evil," only increased as my new, nonacademic community grew, because com-munity cannot flourish without the virtues of temperance, justice, fortitude, humility, faith, hope, and love, and none of these qualify as true virtues without the clear vision of prudence behind them.

Prudence fosters honest humility in a society that valorizes self-confidence, no matter how empty.

What does prudence look like in today's world? First, it provides the ultimate reality check for those of us who have been formed by a fantasy-driven culture. It focuses on the real, including the actuality of good and evil; it pre-vents us from casting ourselves as the heroes of our own private epics; and it helps us stay focused on the Christian cosmos instead of the mirror.

Second, prudence fosters honest humility in a society that valo-rizes self-confidence, no matter how empty. "The bright realm of free human action, dominated by knowledge," Pieper reminds us, "is bordered on all sides by darkness, by the darkness of nature's part within ourselves and by the deeper, impenetrable darkness of the immediate divine governance of our volition and our actions."[31] Though Scripture says this darkness is not darkness at all but really "unapproachable light" (1 Timothy 6:16), to us, as we struggle to come to a decision, it can seem like total obscurity. Prudence allows us to wait in hope for an answer without impulsively trying to "solve things" before they are ready to be solved.

Third, prudence provides the "brave boldness to make final decisions"—this in a culture that does not like to close off options.[32] Yet the ability to decide upon a course of action and then stick to it is critical in every area of life, and particularly for leaders. Even more important, because prudence nails itself to reality, it holds us to the truth and thus ensures that our decisions will be motivated by loving wisdom rather than expediency or egoism.

However, as Pieper reminds us, "there is no 'technique' of the good, no 'technique' of perfection." Growth in prudence "takes place in the course of our replies, appropriate to each given case, to the reality outside us, which is not made by ourselves." In other words, there is no fast track to wisdom. We come to have prudence through our willingness to attend, to listen, to pray, to deliberate, to ponder, to wait, to pass judgment, and then to act—regardless of how much pain a particular decision might cause us.[33]

The somewhat "organic" quality of prudence's development within us can cause its own problems, however. Since there are no techniques we can employ to speed it along, we may be tempted to stop worrying about it and let nature take its course. I find that I am most quickly tripped up in regard to this key virtue by simply failing to think of it at all. On a day-to-day basis, most decisions are not critical ones. Rather than taking the time to think these through in a consciously prudent way, I tend to rely instead on life experience and psychological insight. No big deal, I tell myself—I've been down this road before. No need for spiritual cross-checking this time around.

Yet it is the accumulation of hundreds of small daily choices that ultimately determines whether a life has been lived for God or for oneself. Thus, I am learning to watch for the clues that I am once again sidestepping prudence in order to do it "my way."

First, I check my emotional pulse. Am I metaphorically snorting with self-righteous indignation or panting with anticipatory glee? Am I wriggling with impatience or yawning with boredom? In such cases, prudence has no chance; these strong emotions, or "upheavals of thought," are the key that I've already made up my mind.[34] Second, I take another look at the facts of the situation. More often than not, I discover that I've missed a couple of important points. In my rush to make a decision and move on, I've failed to really listen and take heed. Third, I ask myself a tough two-part question, one that I would rather avoid: Am I either prejudiced or projecting in this case? Am I being swayed by a sense of darkness that might actually be self-created? Last of all, I look back to see if I've prayed about this issue. If I haven't, the danger of acting imprudently is greatly increased.

Trying to live at this level of awareness can feel exhausting at times, especially in a culture that so values spontaneity and impulsiveness. Moreover, sometimes prudence calls for a decision that requires real sacrifice. Yet such willingness to suffer for truth's sake is an aspect of love. And thus prudence becomes one of the ways we live out Christ's double commandment, to love God with all our heart and soul and to love our neighbor as ourself. The good news is that when we sincerely try to do this, when we pray constantly for prudence in our dealings with one another, then grace upon grace is poured out on us.

Basil experienced this grace and rejoiced in it: "We pray always for the face of God to shine upon us, in order that we may be in a state becoming to a holy person, gentle and untroubled in every way, because of our readiness for the good."[35]

Christ said it this way: "If you hold to my teaching, you are really my disciples. Then you will know the truth, and the truth will set you free" (John 8:31–32).

TEMPERANCE

THE ART OF HOLDING A BALANCE

It is by a wonderful divine benevolence that he
who seeks contemplation with a perfect heart, is
occupied in serving others.
St. Gregory the Great (c. 540–604)[1]

Our oldest daughter, Andrea, was finally marrying her Josh, and the wedding countdown was on. Only four months left till July, when 225 guests would be arriving at our place for the nuptial ceremony and feast. Thank heavens I was done with teaching! How else could I handle all that needed to be done?

"Such as?" Mike asked warily.

"Such as . . . well, we need to get a real meadow going out there in the horse pasture. You know, sweet peas and wildflowers and poppies? And we need to finally landscape the backyard, and paint the house, inside and out, and put on a new roof, and—"

"A new *roof*?"

"Well, we need to do it anyway, don't we? We might as well get it done *in time for the wedding.*"

This phrase was uttered in a hushed, awestruck tone. Our daughter was getting married; the whole upcoming event had taken on the air of the sacrosanct as far as I was concerned. How could we possibly quibble over a new roof? "Couldn't you get the guys to help out?" I asked innocently. "The guys"—or "the chain-saw gang," as I usually thought of them—were a band of neighborhood men who weren't happy unless they had something to build, repair, or cut down.

Mike looked dubious, then thoughtful. It *would* be nice to get that dumb roof out of the way. And what better excuse than a wedding?

I spotted the subtle change in expression that signaled he'd taken the hook. Then I said—airily, as though the decision had already been made—"How about green shingles this time, like the ones on the barn?"

His eyes brightened and I knew the hook was set, because he was as big a sucker as his wife for creative projects. Like me, he was helpless before beauty. And hardly ever did we count the physical and mental cost ahead of time. Instead, we visualized, we briskly knocked down doubts, we fed each other's enthusiasm. There would be a freshly painted house, inside and out, and a new roof with green shingles that matched the barn. And a meadow with sweet peas. Not to mention, of course, the wedding preparations themselves. And all of this in the next four months.

I went to the hardware store and bought paint—nine different colors. Three would go outside, and the other six (I could already see this so clearly in my mind) would go inside the house: different colors for different walls *in the same room*. Why hadn't I thought of this before? For years we'd been putting up with this bland and boring whiteness. Now we would have color, a virtual riot of it—color that would match the wildflowers in our new meadow!

"How," Mike remembered to ask me a few weeks later as I wearily climbed down from my paint-spotted ladder, "are we going to keep this proposed meadow going all the way to July? This is California, remember? We're going to be out of rain in about six days."

I stared at him balefully, as though the climate were somehow his fault, and raised an aching shoulder. "We've got to irrigate—that's all there is to it."

"Irrigate an acre and a half of wildflowers? All the way to July?"

I nodded soberly.

He shrugged and went out to locate the Rain Bird sprinkler heads we hadn't used since the passing of our horse-and-sheep phase nearly ten years before. I was climbing back up the ladder, this time with a pail of burnt orange paint called "Flowerpot," when he came puffing back up the hill. "We're missing six," he said. "I'm going down to the hardware store. And don't forget: tomorrow the guys are starting on the roof. I told them breakfast at 7:00."

The guys! I'd forgotten all about the guys! The beautiful new green shingles were stacked in the driveway and all the tools were laid out, but somehow I'd failed to store up food supplies for this gang of big men who ate like a pack of lumberjacks. I climbed back down the ladder, pounded the paint lid back on the bucket of Flowerpot, and went to the hose to wash up. They'd be eating at our house for the next five mornings at least. I needed Canadian bacon, sausage links, many more dozen eggs than our chickens could possibly produce in the coming few hours, buttermilk for pancakes, pinto beans, salsa . . .

Later that afternoon I dragged in with the shopping bags, passing on my way a dried-out orange paintbrush. How could I have forgotten to stick it in a coffee can of water? "Mike," I called, "are you home? Because I think you need to get down to the hardware store again."

At the two-month mark, the green shingles were on, the orange paint glowed bravely on one hallway wall (I'd decided to concentrate on the exterior of the house first), and the sweet peas were struggling manfully against major climatic odds. Morning after morning I moved the Rain Birds down the line by hand before trudging back up the hill to once again don my painting clothes. Mike, meanwhile, was trying to build a dance floor in the middle of the meadow while somehow avoiding the gaily splashing sprinklers. We'd made some progress, that was clear, but everywhere I looked I saw more things that needed to be done. And we were running rapidly out of time. How had this *happened*?

Though I was too tired right then to face up to it, I knew very well what had happened. We were once again caught up in the creative mania that got us every time. We were doing what we'd always done, both singly and together: we were flying high on the creative energy of eros. Despite all the changes we'd made in our life—despite the genuinely contemplative turn it had taken—we had somehow fallen back into the old eros-dominated mind-set that invariably ran us into the ground.

Good Desire Gone Berserk

Eros is a longing desire that can't be assuaged. Though we often think of eros as just another name for sexual desire, the erotic force within us is far greater than sex. Eros is what fuels human creativity, intellectual discovery, and even religious seeking. What eros wants, however, can never be found in its entirety. The British Romantic poets pictured the object of eros as an ever-receding horizon we can never reach, despite all our striving. This unreachability is part and parcel of eros. It propels us urgently toward a place at which we will never arrive. This inescapable fact about erotic desire is central to Plato's view of the human condition: Diotima in the *Symposium* characterizes the daemon Eros as needy and poor, "tough, squalid, shoeless, and homeless, always lying on the ground without a blanket or a bed, sleeping in doorways and along waysides in the open air."[2] It is this neediness of eros—the yearning for what it does not have—that generates so much energy. Sometimes this force gets channeled into romantic love, sometimes into wild, earthy sex. And sometimes it becomes the impetus for art, science, and philosophy; according to Diotima, eros at its higher levels is about "engendering and bringing to birth in the beautiful."[3]

Building on Plato, philosopher Iris Murdoch says that "carnal love [eros] teaches that what we want is always 'beyond', and it gives us an energy which can be transformed into creative virtue."[4] Yet "we cannot acquire and assimilate the beautiful," no matter how we want to; it is "in this instructive sense transcendent."[5] Putting it in Christian terms, the true function of eros, whether in its sexual or creative aspect, is to propel us not toward sex or beauty for its sake alone, but always toward the holy.

Father Ronald Rolheiser writes out of this Christian tradition regarding eros in his popular book *The Holy Longing*. Here, erotic desire is an "unquenchable fire, a restlessness, a longing, a disquiet ... a wildness that cannot be tamed, a congenital all-embracing ache that lies at the center of human experience."[6] "Spirituality," he declares, "concerns what we do with [this] desire. It takes its root in the eros inside of us and it is all about how we shape and discipline that eros."[7]

Erotic energy requires restraint if it is not to destroy us. Says Rolheiser, "All energy is imperialistic, especially erotic and creative energy. Energy is not friendly, it wants all of us, it can beat us up like the playground bully."[8] Worse, it can lay us open to spiritual forces we can't resist. As British Romantic Mary Shelley so brilliantly demonstrates in her famous story of Victor Frankenstein, creative mania can lead to madness, mayhem, and even death.[9]

Though our nine different colors of paint and the acre and a half of sweet peas seemed pretty benign in comparison to the horror that emerged from Frankenstein's laboratory, it was true that we

were being tyrannized by our own creative energy and were wearing out in the process. Everything else was being shoved to the
side, including my usual spiritual routine of early morning reading,
prayer, walking, meditation, and Mass. The hoped-for results of our
hard labor, visualized over and over again, were far too compelling.
There had to be a way—a virtue, perhaps?—that would allow us to
manage and appropriately channel our beauty-loving eros.

I took a day off and went to the hermitage. There, the familiar
routine of the bells, of monks heading in to church from wherever
they'd been working, of liturgy and prayer somehow broke the
spell. For the first time in months, I was able to step out of the
surging flood tide that had been bouncing me along on its crest. To
my surprise, the world hadn't changed much in my absence. Some
of it—the flickering white candles, the midmorning sun streaming
through the eastern windows, the clarity of Father Isaiah's soaring
tenor during the Benedictus—was utterly beautiful.

And some of it wasn't. One brother's allergies, for example, had
not let up a whit. Another monk, looking more depressed than
usual, was yawning sourly into his cupped hand. When Eucharist
was over and I headed back outside, I found two baby swallows
lying dead beside the door; alone in the mud nest above them,
their overgrown sibling triumphantly puffed his sparse down. It
was clear that there was no overcoming the ugliness of illness, sin,
or the brutal side of nature—at least not through the making of
beauty. Seen in that light, my manic efforts to transform the bit
of world under my purview were laughable. Worse, they smacked
of egoistic fantasy.

Sobered by the thought, I wandered into the bookstore in
search of help. Pinned on the wall was an announcement for a
meeting of the local chapter of Alcoholics Anonymous the following Tuesday evening. I stared, thinking about addiction, about

my inability to get a handle on creative mania, and about my grandmother, who used to sneak out to meetings of the Woman's Christian Temperance Union.

Why Temperance Is a Good Thing

The Woman's Christian Temperance Union. I began to smile. That was it, the name of the virtue I'd been looking for, the virtue that could restrain and channel erotic energy. It was called temperance, and despite the spiritual disciplines I'd practiced over the years—solitude, silence, fasting—which were all intended to reveal the places in me over which desire held sway, I had developed very little of it indeed.

But what exactly was it, this no-longer-talked-about moral muscle known as temperance? I glanced through the bookshelves for a likely title, then trotted back out to the car for Josef Pieper's book on the virtues. The purpose of temperance, I found, is integrative: it "dispose[s] various parts into one unified and ordered whole."[10] Pieper points to St. Paul's description of the intended harmony of the body as the Christian version of this ancient cardinal virtue: "The body is a unit, though it is made up of many parts; and though all its parts are many, they form one body" (1 Corinthians 12:12). In other words, no one part can be allowed to overwhelm or dominate the others, for this would violate the integrity of the whole.

Translated in terms of eros, this means that the problem with obsessive desire, which so easily annihilates everything in its path, is that it inflates one part of us to the detriment of the rest and thus destroys our inner harmony and order.

St. Thomas Aquinas provides a second definition of temperance: "serenity of the spirit." This is not the sort of self-satisfied peaceful contentment that comes from a failure to dig deeply or to look outside our own narrow experience. Neither does it grow out of spiritual laziness or a refusal to be bothered. True serenity of the spirit flows from inner order alone. It is the fruit of what Pieper calls "selfless self-preservation."[11]

Rolheiser believes we ignore the need for temperance at our own peril: "Our culture is too naive about the power of energy. We see nothing wrong in exposing ourselves to it in all its rawness."[12] The consequences of this naiveté are twofold: when we plunge heedlessly after eros, we either become inflated with a false sense of our own power or become frightened and exhausted, back off entirely, and sink into depression.

Pieper agrees with Rolheiser that intemperance is a kind of autoimmune disorder: "the same forces from which human existence derives its being can upset that inner order to the point of destroying the spiritual and moral person."[13] Temperance requires that we pay attention to our inner condition.[14] Just as to a large degree we and we alone are responsible for the health of our own bodies— we can either build them up or destroy them with the food we choose and the exercise we do or don't get—we are also responsible for protecting and conserving our own inner order. This means we cannot afford to cave in to the dark thrill of unrestrained eros.

The serenity of spirit described by Aquinas is diametrically opposed, however, to much contemporary thought about what constitutes the good life. Our modern mind-set is still a romantic one—we tend to reject the terms *temperance* and *moderation* for the same reason we reject prudence: they seem self-protective, overly cautious, even cowardly. Instead, we admire extremists: extreme athletes, rock stars who go out in a drug-induced blaze of glory, movie stars who marry and divorce at will. These people, we think, aren't afraid to live, and they are certainly not afraid of social criticism. They do what they want.

I was once a great admirer of this heedless romantic exuberance, and my ecstatic exploits cost me (and others) a price almost too steep to bear. Now I was no longer intrigued by the image of the romantic hero on his passionate, suicidal trajectory. I *wanted* serenity of spirit; I wanted to be temperate. The only problem was that I had no clue how to redirect old patterns of thinking and behavior.

St. Gregory the Great: Who Blended Creativity with Serenity

Back in the bookstore, I looked around for a saint whose life might be instructive—preferably someone who knew how easy it was to be drawn into creative mania and also had lived both an active and a contemplative life. Hermits need not apply. Then I spotted St. Gregory the Great, one of the most influential of the Bishops of Rome, and one of only two popes to have been declared a doctor of the church.

Here was a man whose creative vision outstripped our field of sweet peas by a mile. Yet despite his far-flung projects, one of which involved sending missionaries to the mostly pagan island of England, he'd also displayed enough serenity of spirit to be dubbed "the doctor of contemplation."[15] If anyone could teach me about temperance, it had to be him.

Gregory was born about 540 into both an important senatorial family and a tumultuous Italian political scene.[16] The last Western Roman emperor had been toppled less than seventy years before his birth, and the former imperial capital had been ruled by German kings until 535, when Eastern emperor Justinian sent his Byzantine armies in hopes of wresting Rome away from the barbarians.[17] Gregory's growing-up years were thus shaped by the chaos of war; before he turned fifteen, Rome had undergone at least four separate sieges that led to widespread plague and starvation among the populace.[18]

Though his next fifteen years saw comparative peace, in 568 a terrible new force appeared on the northern horizon: a war-loving tribe called the Lombards who had managed to cross the Alps.

Their invasions went on for the rest of the century, and during this time imperial Rome slowly lost even the memory of its glorious past. The church increasingly found itself in the position of maintaining economic and social health by, for example, taking on responsibility for the grain supply, for repairing aqueducts, and for feeding the poor.[19]

Following in his family's footsteps, the multitalented young Gregory served as prefect of the city until the age of thirty-four, when he underwent a dramatic life conversion. He resigned his secular position and set up a monastery, St. Andrew's, on the Caelian Hill in a house inherited by his father. There, he sank into the silence and peace of full-time prayer.[20] As he put it years later in a letter to a friend, "Having left behind what belongs to the world (as I mistakenly thought at the time), I escaped naked from the shipwreck of this life."[21]

His withdrawal was short-lived, however; as the great-grandson of a pope (Felix III), and in light of his impressive education and natural gifts, he was sure to attract the attention of the church. In fact, he was quickly tapped for service by the reigning pontiff, Pelagius II. In 579, he was made the papal legate to Constantinople, a position he occupied for a number of years until his return to Rome, where he served in the diaconate. In 590, he became the new pope.

His yearning for the contemplative tranquility of the monastery never ceased, however, despite his increasing preoccupation with church business, and this note is sounded over and over again in his prodigious writings: "When the mind, divided and torn, is drawn into so many and such weighty matters, when can it return to itself, so as to recollect itself?"[22] Yet at the same time, he understood the highest kind of Christian life to be what was then referred to as "mixed," rather than purely contemplative: a combination of prayer and action. Gregory believed that Christians were clearly meant to be *in* the world, though not *of* it. "We must note that just as the right order of life is to tend from the active to the contemplative; so the soul often reverts profitably from the contemplative to the active, so that the contemplative life having kindled the mind, the active life might be the more perfectly led."[23] He was convinced that all Christians, not just monks or clergy, were called to contemplation and that the duty of preachers and pastors was to feed spiritual growth in this direction through their teaching of the Scriptures: "Those who seek the purity of the contemplative life are to be shown not the ordinary things about the sacred scripture, but rather the higher and more sublime things."[24] These preachers, however, must continually turn to and refresh their own contemplative hearts, or they would not be of any use to their congregations. Biblical knowledge alone was woefully insufficient—pastors must also be people of deep prayer.

Gregory's mixed approach to spiritual growth and transformation led to his acquiring the virtue of temperance, particularly as an administrator. Committed to fostering and protecting the purity of the church, he consistently avoided the temptations of a lawless, greedy era. He forbade simony and insisted that lands unfairly acquired by the clergy be returned to their owners. His official appointments tended to be monks, trained in ascetic discipline, over clerics or laypeople, who were likely to be more easily impressed by power and riches.[25] His self-restraint was all the more remarkable considering the secular power vacuum in Rome at the time and the golden opportunity this might have presented to a different kind of pope, one intent on dominating the political scene.

His temperance was also evident in the delicate and nuanced way he dealt with people on a one-to-one basis. In his *Pastoral Rule*, for example, he points out that the combination of various personality types and different social circumstances makes for complicated human beings, each of whom responds best to individualized treatment. Where a naturally exuberant, warm, and enthusiastic monk might need toning down in order to avoid falling into outright revelry and lechery, a naturally dark, sad, and withdrawn monk might need exactly the opposite: an infusion of hope, inspiration, and a vision of the light.[26]

In other words, one rule cannot possibly work for all. Gregory thought that as Christians we can either help foster inner order and serenity of spirit among our fellow believers or destroy it. When the latter happens, moral zealotry is most often the culprit. Gregory was extremely sensitive to how easily and even naturally we are led astray by the flesh. "We often feel compunction over our misdeeds, yet we return to them after weeping over them."[27] Genuine Christian love recognizes this inherent weakness of ours and does not condemn but seeks instead to strengthen and heal. Real love also leads to the understanding that salvation is ultimately corporate; if we abandon our neighbor, we are in some way responsible for, and even doomed to, the fate he now faces.[28]

Gregory was convinced, as were his desert-dwelling predecessors, that the Christian life is a life of spiritual warfare on an invisible battlefield. The stakes here are the highest: eternity in the kingdom of heaven or everlasting perdition. Those who can see clearly owe help to those who cannot; souls are at stake, and lack of spiritual vision can be deadly. For Gregory, this meant that the saint and the holy man are absolutely essential to the Christian community: "To lesser mortals blinded by the Fall, they reveal the invisible world which is always very much present."[29] It is the role of these mediators between the carnal and the spiritual realms to reveal what they see, no matter how dire the vision and unwelcome the message.

In the same way that we are meant to achieve and then protect our own inner order and serenity of spirit through the virtue of temperance, we are also meant to work for the order and unity of the entire universe, all of which is made by God. Gregory believed that even Satan can be seen as having his place in this cosmos: he is tempter, exactor, the hammer of the Lord. His depredations against us and the world, when seen through the eyes of faith, are not meant to draw us into the darkness but are meant to reflect God's loving desire that we be transformed into new creatures. Because these satanic forays against us cause considerable pain and shame, they can call out of us what Gregory describes as a "humble love we bestow in turn on one another," a love against which Satan is ultimately powerless.[30] Christian love thus helps hold evil in check.

Setting Healthy Limits on Our Frenzy

I set the Gregory book back on the shelf, casting the monk on duty an apologetic look for my hour of absorbed browsing. As I had noticed before, the virtues require the backdrop of the ancient Christian cosmos to fully come into focus. The modern, romantic framework does not provide a set of beliefs that can make sense of setting voluntary limitations on desire. My spurts of creative mania—my compulsion to stay up all night putting the final touches on the six colors in the guest room, for example—were either admirable or a bit eccentric under this modern view of things, not unhealthy or potentially destructive, as the ancients believed. Yet as high-energy, exciting, and momentarily satisfying as my projects usually were, I had to admit that they did indeed suck me out of the world—and away from my contemplative heart.

Our contemporary romantic framework does not provide a set of beliefs that can make sense of setting voluntary limitations on desire.

How could I lovingly respond to an unexpected visitor, for example, when I was caught up in a frenzy of creativity? I could barely tear my focus away from the paint long enough to pant hello. How could I maintain a nourishing routine of sleeping, walking, meditating, reading, and attending Mass when I was obsessed with finishing the job? Even when I tried to pray, I was busily calculating how many square feet the last two buckets of paint would cover. How could I listen for the still small voice of God when my head was pounding so loudly with excitement? I couldn't even hear Mike calling me from the next room.

Seen from this perspective, I could now understand the purpose of temperance. It serves as a silent watchman, protecting what is unified and holy within. It shields us from the gale-force winds of raw energy, winds that can tear us apart. It forces us to think realistically about ourselves and our human limits. And it shows up the "divine egoism" of romanticism for what it really is. The path of unrestrained eros the romantics followed had no end; the horizon kept receding before them, because they were chasing after an alluring, often beautiful, but ultimately illusory goal. And I was too, when caught up in creative mania.

Understanding a new concept and incorporating it into one's life are two different things, however, and it took me awhile to come up with a way to keep track of myself in regard to intemperance. A big part of the problem was that I'd learned to fuel myself on creative mania when I was a very small child, and this had come to seem normal and even necessary to my psychological well-being. How could I make such a dramatic change without ill effects? Would I still be myself without my hyperenergetic creativity?

Naturally, these dire thoughts were mostly just signs of resistance. I already knew why change was required. But where to begin?

Then I had a major realization, applicable to the practice of all the virtues, but very specifically to temperance, the one I needed most at that moment. It was this: virtues grow out of action practiced habitually. They actually usurp other habits, like a hardy ground cover can eventually colonize a field overgrown with crabgrass. Habit building is a slow process in this regard, for the whole landscape has to be changed along the way. And sometimes the simplest method is to place the baby ground cover in small

> *Virtues grow out of action practiced habitually. They actually usurp other habits, like a hardy ground cover eventually colonizes a field overgrown with crabgrass.*

chunks here and there among the crabgrass rather than try to rip those tenacious, tangled strands out ahead of time.

Thus, I began not by halting all creative projects but by deliberately changing my pace. Mania requires speed or it fizzles out, so I started moving more slowly, taking more breaks during the workday, giving thanks for mundane chores like balancing the checkbook that required concentration but not creativity. In the past, such jobs had often seemed like time-wasting obstacles to my "real" work. Now, I found unexpected pleasure in steady, productive labor that served a purpose but had no self-expressive element to it.

Second, I learned to recognize the signs of an impending creative-mania attack. The moment I found myself obsessively thinking about how a gardening project would look when it was done, or the moment excitement-generated insomnia struck in regard to a prospective new book, I understood that I was in danger. If I didn't plug the dam quickly, it was almost impossible to stop the surging floodwaters once they'd broken through. One effective way to plug it was to purposely leave the project unfinished for a while. At first this almost drove me nuts, for at the heart of creative effort sits a magnetic vision of unity and completeness that ceaselessly urges us on, but when I thought about how intemperance fragmented *me*, it became easier to walk away when the need arose.

Finally, I began praying that God would bless each day's work, no matter what it happened to be, which took my efforts out of the personal realm and placed them where they belonged. Learning to see all work, creative or not, as participation in the divine life took the starch out of romantic "divine egoism" and helped break my addiction to the artist's high. Slowly I began to feel in its place the quiet but steady energy that accompanies internal order.

Without such order, we can do little for God. With it, we can finally begin to understand and respond to these mysterious words of Peter: "Prepare your minds for action; be self-controlled; set your hope fully on the grace to be given you when Jesus Christ is revealed. As obedient children, do not conform to the evil desires you had when you lived in ignorance. But just as he who called you is holy, so be holy in all you do; for it is written: 'Be holy, because I am holy'" (1 Peter 1:13–16).

3

FORTITUDE

THE ART OF COURAGEOUS CONTINUING

*Not learning but anointing teaches it; it is not
grasped by knowledge but by conscience.*
St. Bernard of Clairvaux (1091–1153)[1]

The wedding was over, the bride and groom off on their honey-
moon, the guests long dispersed. Left behind were the dozens of
bronze handbells with which we'd rung in the new marriage, the
green shingles on the roof, and the stacked planks of the disman-
tled dance floor. The meadow was gone, its riot of orange poppies
and lavender sweet peas and white fava bean blossoms now mowed
to a dry stubble. The days of feasting had ended; we were back in
ordinary time.

At first it was a relief and a luxury: it had been glorious, but
we were exhausted. For a couple of nights running, I fell into a
deep, dreamless sleep the moment my head hit the pillow. On the
third night, however, I closed my eyes, tucked a foot around Mike's
ankle, and began to drift off, only to be immediately wrenched
back into wide-eyed wakefulness. Within moments, I was once
again in the middle of it, the chilling terror with no name that
had been stalking me for several years now. The four-month bout
of creative mania, however spiritually unhealthy it may have been,

had at least provided a compelling distraction. But now the darkness was back, more powerfully than ever.

I lay rigid, mentally shivering, trying not to think. Thinking made things more complicated, producing images I couldn't later shake. I could feel Mike's ankle beneath my foot; it was lean, scratchy, and giving off reassuring little jerks. I squeezed closer to the warm length of him, but this only made the fear worse. For the void was once again yawning open beneath our second-floor window. This whirling vortex would eventually suck into it everything I loved and cared about. My heart was sinking, my temperature dropping, the cool mist of terror invading my lungs.

What, I thought desperately, had Father Isaiah taught me to do at times like this? Yes, that was it: to cross myself, to hug myself, to pray for the light. I tried to bend my fingers into position and got nowhere. But that was the way this darkness worked, and why it was so frightening. Prayer got numbed. You couldn't even cry out for help, because suddenly God had vanished. And you were paralyzed, unable to resist the demon of futility, whose venom worked like hemlock: first the body went cold, feet to neck, and then the mind. Where to turn? What to do?

I lay trembling for nearly an hour this time before it passed, and I lay awake the rest of the night thinking somber, hopeless thoughts. How could the Orthodox sing so triumphantly about Christ trampling down death? Death reigned everywhere. Where was the hope? Where was the glory? It was all going to bone and ash in the end. Why pretend? Why pray? Why even continue to live? Living was *hard*, and in the end, death made a mockery of everything.

These bouts of darkness were debilitating for several days afterward. Forget about creativity; most times I couldn't even work up energy to cook or do dishes. The spiritual breath had been knocked out of me; the injury was real. Safe in the light of day, I would cast sullen, barbed, wordless thoughts God's way. Where did he go during those times? How could he just abandon me like that? Didn't he understand how eviscerating it was for a simple human creature to go through that kind of terror?

Then one day St. Thomas Aquinas helped me figure out at least part of what was happening during these dreadful moments. When we love anything on this earth, he said, and when we begin to understand at a bone-deep level just how ephemeral those things we love are—when we achieve a "truly penetrating knowledge of created things"—then we are subject to "an abysmal sadness, an insuperable sadness which cannot be lifted by any natural force of knowledge or will."[2]

Though I had felt more fear than sorrow during these struggles with the dark side, I did agree with Aquinas that at the bottom of these experiences lay inconsolable grief at the fleeting nature of physical life. Not that I hadn't intellectually grasped this truth long before; I'd been teaching literature for years, after all, and great literature faces this awful fact head-on. But for the first time, I was living within this reality rather than merely thinking about it. In order to follow that faint but unmistakable contemplative call of a few years back, I'd left behind a career, a certain kind of social standing, a lot of youthful dreams about who and what I would be someday. My world was smaller now, and more intensely focused, which made everyone in it that much more precious to me.

Yet the bottom line was that I could hang on to none of it, not even the little portion I'd managed to hide away for myself: Mike, the kids, my writing, our peaceful sanctuary of a home. "All men are like grass," says the prophet Isaiah, "and all their glory is like the flowers of the field. The grass withers and the flowers fall, because the breath of the LORD blows on them" (40:6–7). Like our riotously beautiful wedding meadow, the generations are born, flourish, and die out, most of them leaving behind not even a memory in the hearts of those who follow. How can you know that, I thought, and ever smile again? How can you take that in—let its inevitability sink deeply into your heart—and still believe that life has an ultimate, even triumphant, meaning? It was really too much to bear.

A Journey into Soulful Fear

Each time I went through this valley of the shadow, I was convinced that no other Christian had ever experienced such hell, that there was obviously something terribly weak about my so-called faith. Yet Christians throughout history, many of them far stronger than me, have undergone similar periods of intellectual anguish. Psychologist William James devotes an entire chapter of his famous book *The Varieties of Religious Experience* to this form of existential despair. He says, "The normal process of life contains moments as bad as any of those which insane melancholy is filled with, moments in which radical evil gets its inning and takes its solid turn. The lunatic's visions of horror are all drawn from the material of daily fact."[3] Among his examples, James cites Tolstoy, whose *Confession* describes experiences of nihilism that almost led to suicide just before the famous writer stepped into the light of redemption and grace: "What will be the outcome of what I do today? Of what I shall do tomorrow? What will be the outcome of all my life? Why should I live? Why should I do anything? Is there in life any purpose which the inevitable death which awaits me will not undo?"[4]

As awful as these moments can be, the contemplative tradition insists that some version of the experience of existential dread is an integral part of the journey. Anglican mystic Evelyn Underhill tells us that "the condition of access to higher levels of vitality is a death; a deprivation, a detachment, a clearing of the ground. . . . Even the power of voluntary sacrifice and self-discipline is taken away. A dreadful ennui, a dull hopelessness, takes its place."[5]

Episcopalian priest and psychologist Morton Kelsey says, "Many of the most experienced in the spiritual struggle have told us that the same darkness attacks again and again, and the further we go upon the path, the more subject we become to attack. The victory is not something that occurs once and for all. . . . The Christian Way is indeed a journey with many perils. It is not a safe refuge."[6]

However—and this is a big *however*—"we are not meant to remain in darkness" but instead to "appropriate the victory of Christ and pass through the confrontation again and again."[7] This is the struggle Christ is referring to when he says, "Take up your cross and follow me," and this was what Father Isaiah had been trying to get across when he taught me to pray for the light. At some level I knew this—knew it was terribly important that I learn to confront rather than reel away from or become paralyzed by these attacks of spiritual darkness—but I had not the courage to stand tall. Not a measly ounce of it. And how was a natural-born, fifty-year-old coward ever to become brave?

Fortitude and Moving Forward

Sighing, I once again dragged out my guide to the virtues and turned to the chapter on fortitude. Much to my surprise, the first line gave me immediate hope. "Fortitude," says Josef Pieper, "presupposes vulnerability."[8] We cannot even *have* this virtue unless we are capable of being injured. The stoic who has so completely detached himself from passion and desire that he is no longer disturbed by anything cannot, under this definition, be considered brave.

Further, our injuries don't have to be physical; they can be "every violation of our inner peace; everything that happens to us or is done with us against our will; . . . everything in any way negative, everything painful and harmful, everything frightening and oppressive."[9] Apparently I'd been laboring under a misapprehension—that I was a coward because I was afraid. Somehow I'd had the notion that the terms *courage, bravery,* and *fortitude* were synonyms for fearlessness and that to develop the virtue of fortitude, I had to stop being frightened. And that was not possible: not with an imagination like mine, anyway.

What did I fear most? That wasn't hard to figure out: "The ultimate injury, the deepest injury, is death." The most horrifying aspect of these attacks of spiritual darkness is the pervading sense that death triumphs in the end and that hope is a comforting illusion that must give way to this cold reality. Yet despite our natural human aversion to death, fortitude requires that we meet it head-on; fortitude "is basically readiness to die, or, more accurately, readiness to fall, to die, in battle."[10]

More, the "essential and the highest achievement of fortitude is martyrdom, and readiness for martyrdom is the essential root of all Christian fortitude."[11] I couldn't even sustain a simple cooking burn without whimpering. There was no way I could bravely climb onto a pyre of dry sticks about to explode into flame. I worried about this lack of zeal. What if we were invaded someday? What if I were ordered to deny my faith or suffer some excruciating death? Would I toss aside the beliefs that gave my life meaning the moment things got tough?

Of course I would. If I tried to rely for one minute on my own resources, it was all over. Only the "overflowing grace of God," which can "lift the soul with exceeding strength to things divine," could prevent my collapse into mindless terror should I ever be put to the martyr test. My job was simply to cling to God no matter what. Martyrdom is not something you can practice for. In fact, the ancient church frowned heavily on those who voluntarily turned themselves over to the oppressors; these eager beavers appeared to be motivated by prideful fantasy rather than Christian virtue.[12]

But martyrdom represents the extreme. Less dramatic but still genuine tests of bravery come along on a daily basis. I thought about my own life and realized how often vainglory, rather than fortitude, was operational at these times. In smugly standing up to a bureaucratic bully, or self-righteously giving an audience a piece of my mind, I'd more often than not been mistaking self-assertion for courage.

The virtue of fortitude cannot coexist with egoistic strutting. Fortitude is as dependent upon our having a clear vision of the good as any of the other cardinal virtues. Only the person who is both prudent and just can be truly courageous.[13] "It is for the sake of the good," says Aquinas, "that the brave man exposes himself to the danger of death."[14] It is not, as modern people are apt to believe, for the sake of self-esteem—in order to think well of oneself.

In smugly standing up to a bureaucratic bully, or self-righteously giving an audience a piece of my mind, I'd more often than not been mistaking self-assertion for courage.

More, fortitude is not limited to battlefield heroism but is also found in patient endurance of evil for the sake of good. Given circumstances we cannot possibly change or resist, courage means that we endure without being defeated. As Aquinas puts it, "The patient man is not the one who does not flee from evil, but the one who does not allow himself to be made inordinately sorrowful thereby."[15] Endurance as an aspect of fortitude comes from a "vigorous grasping of and clinging to the good."[16] We understand that our suffering, like Christ's, is not passive but an active refusal to capitulate to evil.

I realized that I did not have to be a natural-born hero to acquire the virtue of fortitude—I simply had to cling to the good and call on God for the grace to either "pounce" upon evil when necessary or (more likely in this fallen world where evil often seems overwhelmingly powerful) patiently endure it without allowing it to grind me into powder. But I had not yet found something to help me stand up under those bouts of spiritual darkness—not until I came to Aquinas's concept of the "purgatorial" dimension of fortitude, which is what "gives the soul the power to remain undaunted by its entrance into the higher world."[17]

About our entry into the spiritual realm, Teresa of Ávila says, "I assert that an imperfect human being needs more fortitude to pursue the way of perfection [contemplation] than to suddenly become a martyr." St. John of the Cross experienced the gradual penetration into the world of spirit as a series of "dark nights"—the dark night of the senses, the dark night of the soul. Pieper says, "The Christian who dares to take the leap into this darkness and relinquishes the hold of his anxiously grasping hand, totally abandoning himself to God's absolute control, thus realizes in a very strict sense the nature of fortitude; for the sake of love's perfection he walks straight up to dreadfulness."[18]

St. Bernard of Clairvaux: Who Modeled Visionary and Spiritual Strength

How can we learn to face the depths of spiritual mystery in this simple, trustful way? The saints can act as our guides. I thought about the contemplative monk who once preached a disastrous Crusade—Bernard of Clairvaux—and the lesson in fortitude he might offer me.

Bernard was born into the predawn light of the twelfth century, often considered to be the high point of medieval Christian spirituality. A hundred years before his 1091 birth date,[19] Europe was still struggling out of the Dark Ages that followed the final collapse of the

Roman Empire in the West. A hundred years after his death in 1153, the University of Paris—a new European phenomenon that provided the seedbed for secular humanism—was already well established. He lived to see the first indications of a great shift in Western thought, and much of his work was devoted to preserving and strengthening the high medieval vision of the Christian cosmos.[20]

Not much is known about his early life, despite the fact that a "vita," or saintly biography, was already in the works long before he died. He was born in a fortified castle in Fontaine-les-Dijon, Burgundy, the son of a knight and expected to follow in his father's footsteps. However, instead of being trained like his brothers for a military career, Bernard was educated at a school called Saint-Vorles, which was run by canons regular, or religious brothers. He did well in his studies, which gave him the foundation for his later accomplishments as a profound thinker and brilliant Latin stylist.[21]

In his early twenties he began to seriously consider becoming a monk, though not the sort of monk found in the great Benedictine houses of Cluny. The Cluniac communities had become more and more focused on liturgical grandeur and had lost much of the connection to manual labor, silence, and solitude that had typified earlier monasticism. A general movement toward monastic reform in the late eleventh century had sent people into the forests of Italy, France, and northern England to once again take up the simple hermit life of the early desert fathers. The goal was an environment more conducive to contemplation.

Less than twenty years before Bernard's birth, a group of hermits not far from Langres, France, invited an abbot called Robert to govern them. They cut down trees, built huts, and settled into community life. By 1098, when Bernard was a child of seven, the group had split, with twenty of them restarting the experiment in the forest of Cîteaux, not far from Bernard's family home in Burgundy.[22]

As a teenager, he was impressed by their commitment to a simple and austere life of contemplation. In 1113, he made up his mind to join them, bringing with him a group of noble companions that included his brothers and one of his uncles. He was twenty-two, and these were his first converts to monasticism.[23] His devotion to the monk's life was contagious, and within two years he was sent out to found and direct a daughter house, Clairvaux, in Champagne. In 1119, Pope Calixtus II confirmed the charter written by the third abbot of Cîteaux, and the growing community officially became an order.[24] These white-robed monks called the Cistercians would live under the original, unmitigated Rule of St. Benedict, do their own manual labor, and avoid all fiscal entanglements.[25]

Bernard devoted the balance of his life to creating new Cistercian houses around Europe, 68 of them within the next thirty-five years. By the time he died, his order owned 350 monasteries inhabited by tens of thousands of monks and extending from Scandinavia to Portugal. He had some hand in the ongoing administration of nearly half of these.[26]

Right from the beginning, however, he dedicated himself to spiritually guiding the monks under his care. In 1124, his prior requested a written version of his doctrine on humility, a work that became his first great treatise, *The Steps of Humility and Pride*. In the preface, he describes the soul-searching he underwent before agreeing to take on the job. "I wanted to do justice to your [Brother Godfrey's] request (Mk 15:15), as it deserved, but I feared that it would be beyond me. I was not able to find the boldness to begin until I had remembered the Gospel's advice (Lk 14:28) and then I sat down and counted up to see whether I had enough resources to complete it. Love conquered my fear (1 Jn 4:18) that I should not be able to finish the work (Lk 14:30)."[27]

Once he had decided to write the text, he met with new doubts:

Then another fear swept me from the opposite direction, I began to fear that I should stand in a greater danger of pride if I did complete it than of ignominy if I failed. There I was at the cross-roads, hesitating long between fear and love, undecided to which road I might more safely commit myself, fearing either to try to speak profitably of humility when I should myself be found lacking in it, or to keep silent and be found useless. And since I saw that neither road was safe, but I had to take one or the other, I chose to do what I could to bring you the fruit of my talk rather than to lurk for my own safety in the harbor of silence.[28]

The difficulty Bernard describes in this passage is a common one—should I or shouldn't I step into this new role I'm being offered? Am I making this decision on the basis of egoism or obedience? Given the morally and spiritually demanding monastic climate in which he lived, Bernard was being asked to take the risk of extreme public embarrassment. What if he wrote a treatise on humility and thereby revealed, in print, a monstrous pridefulness to which he himself was blind? As a respected leader within the order, he would be putting his personal reputation on the line, but he went ahead with the project regardless.

In this work, Satan represents pride taken to its furthest point, and Bernard addresses the devil directly:

You too, Satan, were made in the likeness of God, and you had a place not even in the Garden of Eden but in the delights of God's paradise (Ez 28:12). What more ought you to ask? Full of wisdom and perfect in beauty, "Do not seek what is too high and try to look into what is too mighty for you" (Sir 3:22). . . . You want to distinguish yourself from others. You want to pry with your curiosity. You want to push in disrespectfully. You want to set up a throne for yourself in heaven so that you may be like the Most High (Is 14:4).[29]

In twelfth-century Burgundy, Satan was still vividly real. It was an era during which, as the writer Andrew Delbanco puts it, "the air was thought to be so thick with demons that a needle dropped from heaven would have to pierce one on its way down."[30] During Bernard's day, Satan was "a brilliant presence in the illuminated manuscripts and mosaics and oils—a semi-human creature with the features of a dog, or a half-ape, or sometimes . . . a human figure with tail or horns."[31] It took considerable courage to mock the devil in writing.

Bernard's fortitude also manifested itself in his endurance of the long separations from Clairvaux caused by his involvement in ecclesial projects. He was first and foremost a monk, regardless of his influential role in the church of his day, and he longed for the peace of the monastery. The bishop Anselm of Havelberg once met him in Rome and paints a vivid picture of the famous abbot of Clairvaux: in his "coarse habit, and emaciated by mortification," he sat among the clerics of the Vatican, "interpreting and clarifying the words of the Holy Scriptures." Says Anselm, it was clear that "he was in all respects a virtuous man of God; not a pretender, but a genuine disciple of the blessed Benedict."[32]

In a letter written to his brother monks, Bernard admits to being "almost impatient, that I am forced to live without you. It is a long tribulation and a tedious waiting, to remain so long a slave to the affairs of this empty life."[33] A little over a decade later, after preaching the dismally failed Second Crusade, Bernard writes to the prior of a Carthusian monastery, "May my monstrous life, my bitter conscience, move you to pity. I am the chimera of my age, neither cleric nor layman. I have kept the habit of a monk, but I have long ago abandoned the life."[34] Despite his bewildering sense of loss, however, Bernard continued to obediently endure what was most painful for him—separation from the beloved place he called "Jerusalem" and the community he'd been part of since his youth.

Bernard was one of the busiest churchmen of his day, but his response to the contemplative call was ongoing and bore fruit in long nights of prayer and major mystical treatises. In his commentaries on the Song of Songs, a twenty-year project, he traces out man's spiritual journey toward union with God, or the "extension of the relationship of love that exists among and unites the three divine Persons."[35] The soul that is purified through humility and the practice of the virtues has been made ready for the "kiss," or the "presence of the grace of the Incarnate Word" within it.[36] For the kiss to happen, however, "the soul must be alone, free even of intelligent thoughts; everything, even neighborly concern, is put aside and the soul and its spouse are alone."[37]

What pulls us along this mysterious path that lies beyond thought? Bernard says it is desire, "*the* form that love takes in our earthly existence."[38] By "desire," he is referring to the same eros that so often tripped me up before I discovered the virtue of temperance—eros, the source of both creative mania and passionate sexuality.

One of Bernard's great contributions to the Christian tradition is a deep respect for what is uniquely human in the spiritual interchange between God and humanity. For Bernard, we are first and foremost embodied spirits, creatures of flesh, and we have been given our natures for good reason. Thus, our natural affections are not to be suppressed or denied but instead transformed through grace and virtue. Hearts cleansed of self-interest and focused on the living Christ are freed up to love in joyful thanksgiving, to love without fear.[39] For Bernard, Jesus' "double commandment"—to love God with all one's heart and soul and mind and to love one's neighbor as oneself—does not refer to dryly doing one's duty. As we fall deeper and deeper into love with God, we also fall in love with our fellow human beings.

Despite his seemingly optimistic humanism, Bernard was realistic about the limitations of our natural condition. He writes in modern-sounding, matter-of-fact terms about the sense of alienation, despair, dread, futility, and absurdity that is inescapable for thinking mortal beings and can destroy the will to live. However, he believed that the moment we confront the stark reality of our own finitude is the moment we set foot on the spiritual path. This is our internal struggle: to face our condition squarely, which leads to humility, and then to go on in hope, which gives birth to Christian fortitude. "Misery," says Bernard, calls upon "mercy." Or, in other words, existential dread moves us straight into the arms of the Father.[40]

Staking Our Life on Love

Here, finally, seemed to be an insight into those dark nights I'd been going through. First, I was more than likely not under some kind of attack but instead suffering spiritual growing pains. Only after a visceral experience of the godless universe can most of us begin to grasp the full meaning of salvation. The philosopher Pascal, for example, was a nominal Catholic until the day he began to seriously ponder death. He realized how often even those of us who call ourselves believers "run heedlessly into the abyss after putting something in front of us to stop us seeing it."[41] The "easy" option of atheism, when taken to its end point, suddenly makes the full ramifications of the religious choice snap into focus. We can no longer go about our daily business as though there is no tomorrow; we must take a stand, one way or the other. We can either move deeper into the darkness of egoism and self-regard or reorient ourselves toward the light. If we cling fiercely to God throughout, we are strengthened rather than destroyed by this journey.

Second, these experiences of spiritual darkness had opened my eyes, no matter how briefly, to my true self. As Pascal points out, it is rare that we see ourselves as we are. Instead, we "strive constantly to embellish and preserve our imaginary being, and neglect the real one."[42] The dark night shakes us out of our usual complacency and gives us a glimpse of our naked selves. The vision can send us reeling.

Theologian Rudolf Otto calls this insight an experience of "creature-consciousness," or the "emotion of a creature, submerged and overwhelmed by its own nothingness in contrast to that which is supreme above all creatures."[43] For Bernard, the possibility of contemplative knowledge begins at this very place. When we make this "inward-looking glance of self-judgment, as clear and searching as possible," we are forced to confess our own utter inadequacy.[44] Yet if we refuse to cave in to hopelessness and instead stake our lives on the love of the mysterious and powerful Almighty, we are given a glimpse of grace at work within us. This "explains the profound optimism of the Christian who, having taken the measure of his condition, does not yield to despair."[45]

Third, these experiences of darkness had opened me up to a new way of seeing—or, more accurately, *not* seeing—God. Benedictine prioress Mary Margaret Funk writes about the three traditional renunciations required of monks: "First, we must renounce our former way of life and move closer to our heart's desire, toward the interior life. Second, we must do the inner work (of asceticism) by renouncing our mindless thoughts. . . . Third, and finally, we must renounce our own images of God so that we can enter into contemplation of God as God."[46] In other words, we must give up our natural human longing to understand what is beyond our capacity to do so. If we do not, we risk worshipping an idol.

Rudolf Otto says, "The truly 'mysterious' object is beyond our apprehension and comprehension, not only because our knowledge has certain irremovable limits, but because in it we come upon something inherently 'wholly other', whose kind and character are incommensurable with our own, and before which we therefore recoil in a wonder that strikes us chill and numb."[47] Bernard himself, despite his rhapsodic sermons on the loving interaction between God and humans, says of this ultimately incomprehensible Divinity, "He who governs all is all things to all, yet he has no particularities. All that we can say of him in himself is that 'he dwells in inaccessible light' (1 Tm 6:16). His peace is beyond our understanding (Phil 4:7). His wisdom is beyond measure (Ps 146:5) and his greatness has no bounds (Ps 144:3). No man can see him and live (Ex 33:20)."[48]

To experience the complete otherness of God in this way is to tremble. Yet this obscurity, no matter how disconcerting, can open us to new spiritual depths. Apophatic contemplation, with its requirement that we give up all our comforting ideas and favorite mental pictures of the divine, has been practiced throughout the Christian ages, particularly within Eastern Orthodoxy, but also by such Western mystics as the anonymous author of the *Cloud of Unknowing*, St. John of the Cross, and St. Teresa of Ávila.[49] In a sense, it keeps us honest—if we approach God in this way, we cannot be tempted into making him in our own image. But the apophatic way of imageless contemplation can be terrifying and even spiritually dangerous if we are not otherwise supported by firm belief, a sacramental structure that includes frequent Eucharist and ongoing spiritual direction.

During my bouts of spiritual darkness, some of this structure was in place, though certainly not enough. My Christian belief was still relatively weak. I'd spent nearly twenty years of my adult life calling myself an atheist, and this way of thinking had worn certain ruts in me. I had taught modern abyss-focused literature for over a decade; I was used to seeing this awful vision of darkness described in beautiful, alluring language—language I couldn't resist. I had learned to see the void as ultimate. The demon of futility had taken hold in me without my knowing it. When I returned to Christianity in my late thirties, I came wounded, both morally and intellectually. These dark nights had shown me where I was still vulnerable in my faith.

> *Yet those bouts of spiritual darkness had taught me why, and I could not ignore the lesson: to move safely through the spiritual realm, we need both the fortifying nourishment of the sacraments and the loving support of the Body of Christ.*

I'd also fallen prey to a particular temptation of the contemplative life: consistently choosing solitude and silence over corporate church life. Mornings at home were beautiful—if I arose early enough, I could sit on my bench under the pines, meditate in the top of the barn, read for an hour if I chose. I reveled in my freedom. Morning Mass interrupted this lovely quiet time. More, I had to get in the car and drive through early-morning high school traffic to get to the church by 7:00 a.m. The clamoring world never seemed more present than when it honked impatiently to get past me to the school parking lot. Why even bother to go? Yet those bouts of spiritual darkness had taught me why, and I could not ignore the lesson: to move safely through the spiritual realm, we need both the fortifying nourishment of the sacraments and the loving support of the Body of Christ.

It was no surprise to realize that I hadn't listened to my spiritual director very well either. No: I had listened, but I had not *heard*. All along Father Isaiah had been telling me in so many words that I could not "outthink" the darkness. Instead, I had to learn to call upon Christ immediately, without wasting a moment. "O God, come to my assistance," the monks say first thing at dawn. "O Lord, make haste to help me."

This automatic calling upon Christ for help in all things is what Bernard would characterize as humility: the knowledge of who and what we are and—more—what we are *not* capable of doing on our own. Out of this humility comes the possibility of Christian fortitude. No longer are we depending on our own natural resources, but instead we are "firmly grasping and clinging to the good" while at the same time surrendering ourselves to providence. Under these circumstances, we will be filled with God's promised grace, even the grace to undergo martyrdom.

> Out of humility comes the possibility of Christian fortitude. No longer are we depending on our own natural resources but are "firmly grasping and clinging to the good" while surrendering ourselves to providence.

Paul, who in his letter to the Ephesians refers to himself as an "ambassador in chains" for "the mystery of the gospel" (6:19–20), speaks in this way about Christian fortitude: "Finally, be strong in the Lord and in his mighty power. Put on the full armor of God so that you can take your stand against the devil's schemes. For our struggle is not against flesh and blood, but against the rulers, against the authorities, against the powers of this dark world and against the spiritual forces of evil in the heavenly realms. Therefore put on the full armor of God, so that when the day of evil comes, you may be able to stand your ground" (Ephesians 6:10–13).

JUSTICE

THE ART OF FORGIVING

Holiness or purity is due to the virtues which deal with the
passions that obstruct the limpidity of our reason. And peace
is caused by justice, the virtue concerned with our deeds . . .
inasmuch as someone who refrains from wronging other
people removes the occasion for litigation and disturbances.
And in this way the moral virtues prepare the way for the
contemplative life inasmuch as they cause peace and purity.
St. Thomas Aquinas (c. 1225–74)[1]

The Colorado family reunion was history by now, and I was long over my season of misanthropy. Yet something still rankled; whenever the clan got together, something made me feel like a cat backed into a damp corner. And I thought I knew what it was: my sister Gretchen, my "dark" twin, the one sibling out of five who looked like a photographic negative of me.

Our resemblance went deeper than just looks. We were the driven ones in an already hardworking, self-disciplined family. We were the ones who had the most trouble laughing at ourselves. We were the ones who took the quest for holiness very, very seriously indeed. And we were competitive: in fact, for years I'd had the feeling that we were locked in a strange, silent, invisible wrestler's hold that neither of us could break. Yet in spite of our competitiveness, we were also very close. When one was down, the other was generous and available. When one was hurting, the other was always there.

Years earlier, when I finally had to face up to the terrible mess I'd made of my first marriage, I went straight to Gretchen, who sheltered me for several days, listened and gave good counsel, administered a sharp rap on my forehead, and sent me back, strengthened, to deal with my life. Later, when her first child, sixteen-month-old Kirstie, lay comatose in intensive care, I sat beside Gretchen for hours, listening in on the most private of monologues: a mother's last words to her dying baby.

Soon afterward, our paths began to diverge. Gretchen was still in her twenties when her young husband accepted a position in a large Evangelical church in the Midwest, and she took on the role of senior pastor's wife. I, on the other hand, was critically reexamining my childhood faith during this period, eventually repudiating Christianity altogether. This new, seemingly impassable gulf between us was not so much geographical, despite the hundreds of miles that separated our homes, as intellectual and spiritual, especially after I went back to school in my thirties. I couldn't believe I had a minister's wife for a sister; she couldn't believe I'd become so morally and spiritually flippant.

Thus, my unexpected return to Christianity in my early forties both stunned and delighted her. Here, finally, was a way to reconnect. I was more leery than delighted: what I was learning as a brand-new Catholic didn't seem to line up with the beliefs of Evangelicals, who were now becoming such a powerful political force in America. The gulf that should have closed, that *looked* as though it had closed, still lay secretly between us. But this time its effect was more insidious. I noticed, for example, that I was finding it harder and harder to be around her, especially when I was alone. It went beyond simply uncomfortable. I sometimes felt strangely frantic, as though I were stifling and had to get air. I began to wonder if something evil was afoot.

Injustice That Is Personal

Shaken, I went to see Father Isaiah. He asked me to describe my sister, who was about to arrive at our place on the first leg of her family's annual spring visit home. I breathlessly poured out my list of accusations: Proud! Driven! Competitive! Can't brook disagreement! Secretly wants to prove me wrong!

"Well," said Father Isaiah reassuringly, "I certainly don't see anything *evil* here. Troubling, certainly. But I don't think you are being called to do anything special, at least for the moment. Why don't you just pray for calmness, then sort of stay out of her way during this visit? Let things unfold a bit more before you decide what to do?"

This was somewhat disappointing—by now, I was secretly hoping he'd offer to do a long-distance exorcism—but I promised to try my best. I behaved like a ghost the entire time she was at our house. I could see her looking confused—what was going on here?—but she didn't push it. It was only after she'd gone home that she let me know how clearly she was sensing our estrangement. *I feel*, she wrote, *as though somehow I've lost the key to the family home. Can you tell me what I've done wrong?*

Suddenly I was in the middle of a new scene, one that required I step forward and own up to my secret ambivalence about our relationship. Not only that: I was being called to do something about it. But what? How could we possibly open up a conversation about something so vague (not to mention insulting) as my getting the heebie-jeebies whenever I was in her presence?

I checked in with Father Isaiah, who promised to pray for both of us; then I talked to my longtime friend Ken, who advised that Gretchen and I set aside enough time for the prospective conversation—a few days, if possible—in a place where neither of us could just flit home if things got uncomfortable. This was a great idea, if a trifle scary. What would we say to each other for hours and hours? What might come out?

We made arrangements to meet at a Franciscan retreat house in Wisconsin called Solitude Ridge. Each of us would have her own little hermitage with a bed, refrigerator, stove, sink, bathroom, and front porch—a place to recoup when things got too emotional or confusing. We agreed not to call our families while we were together; this time was for the two of us. We also agreed that we would surround everything we did and said with prayer.

Outside the hut in which we met, an icy wind rattled dry cornstalks, and a great blackness had settled over the fields. It was late November in·the Midwest—Gretchen's world—and somehow the two of us sitting cross-legged on the floor in front of the heater seemed to represent the sum total of humanity. I was nervous, mentally armed, and determined to either unlock the mysterious wrestler's hold we'd been in for so long or say good-bye forever. Gretchen was shocked when she realized I might actually sever our relationship for good if things did not work out between us.

Two and a half days later, we emerged from our hermitages, flattened by lack of sleep, hours of intense talk, and—in Gretchen's case—a bad cough and cold. It had been one of the more grueling experiences in both of our lives, one we would never forget. But the gulf had finally been crossed. First, however, we'd had to uncover two deeply buried, long-ago wounds, one on each side, that stemmed from my scandalous behavior during those years away from God. Then we had to forgive each other for, as Gretchen put it, "the sins of our youth, the sins of our middle age, and whatever sins we might accidentally commit against one another in the future."

I got on the plane to California dizzy with wonderment at the dignity, strength, and rocklike faith of this sister I'd wanted exorcised. Sheepishly but happily I called the rest of the family, who had been waiting to hear the outcome of our weekend together. For they had a stake in it too; we were not just two individuals trying to work things out, but also members of a community. And then Gretchen and I hunkered down to tackle the difficult task of building a friendship founded on truth, mutual respect, and the recognition that we were both children of God, despite our many differences.

Unfortunately, this was not the end of the story. Soon enough I was embroiled in yet another relationship crisis, this time with Ken, the very friend who had so helped Gretchen and me by advising our weekend retreat. With this new conflict came the same ambivalence, confusion, defensiveness, and conviction that evil was afoot. For several months I brooded, toying with all sorts of grim theories that might explain my friend's seemingly unloving behavior, including the possibility that he too needed the services of a good exorcist. If only I could locate one (Father Isaiah, I'd come to understand, was not in that particular line of work). Maybe a wily old Jesuit somewhere . . . ?

Instead, I called my new compadre, Gretchen.

"Hmm," she said, when I'd described my state of mind. "Aha. Yes, very interesting indeed."

"*What's* interesting?"

"Can't you see it?"

"See what?"

"The fact that your diagnosis of Ken sounds just like your earlier diagnosis of me?"

Stunned, I held the phone away from my face and stared into the receiver. But of course. This nasty sense of lurking evil was not false at all; evil *was* afoot. Yet I'd completely failed to see where it was coming from: not, as I'd already found out, from Gretchen, and not from my friend Ken. Instead, I was getting whiffs of the rank and rotten miasma that floats around injustice, the failure to give other people their due.

Links between Justice and Judgment

Kant put it this way: "Man's greatest and most frequent troubles depend on man's injustice more than on adversity." Plato took it even deeper: "Any wrong done to me or mine is at once more shameful and worse for the wrongdoer than for me the sufferer." Injustice hurts both parties, but no one more than she who is being unjust. Why?[2]

Justice is firmly rooted in our special identity as spiritual beings who live beyond the limits of the purely physical. Thomas Aquinas saw this personhood of ours as characterized by "freedom, imperishability, and responsibility for the whole of the world."[3] The virtue of justice is what regulates our actions toward our fellow human persons. As Aquinas explains it, "Men relate to each other through external actions . . . ; a man's interior feelings relate him to himself. So justice has as its special field external deeds and objects inasmuch as they relate men to one another."[4]

This focus on the other is what makes justice different from prudence, temperance, and fortitude. Prudence depends on "reason perfected in the clear light of truth"—it is primarily about clarity of vision in regard to the good.[5] Temperance has to do with maintaining internal order. Fortitude is the willingness to persevere for God's sake, regardless of the consequences. Justice, on the other hand, is about what we *do* to one another.

Aquinas uses the term *commutative justice* to describe one person behaving justly toward another, *distributive justice* to describe society behaving justly toward its individual citizens, and *legal justice* to describe a person behaving justly toward the society to which he belongs. Aquinas insists that "justice to individuals . . . excels other virtues: for it perfects our will and not just our feelings; and is not only good for us but good for others: *courage serves others in war, justice serves others in war and in peace.*"[6]

In what way had I been unjust toward Gretchen? I had not physically harmed her, stolen something from her, or damaged her good name (though in my conversations with other family members I may have come close). Aquinas advises that "a man should pick his words carefully, since uttered incautiously they might take away a person's character, and a fatal wrong might be done without even intending it," and I wasn't absolutely sure I'd adhered to that principle.[7]

Even if I'd slipped a little here and there, however, I didn't owe her money and I hadn't cheated her in any way. My injustice toward my sister, and toward Ken, fell into a different category entirely: I had been unjust to both of them in my *judgment*, which is "primarily the definition or determination of what is just."[8]

Aquinas talks about three ways in which judgments can be unjust: when they go against the rightness of justice, extend beyond the judge's authority, or are based on uncertain evidence. I had fallen into all three traps. First, I had come up with the harshest retaliation for being "wronged" that I could think of: the death penalty for these longtime relationships. I had left no room for the possibility of forgiveness and reconciliation. Second, I had passed judgment in areas I knew nothing about; I had condemned my sister and my friend on the basis of what I imagined was going on in the privacy of their hearts and minds. Third, my judgment had been rash—I had leaped to conclusions based on thin evidence.

Was this a pattern for me? Did I regularly pass unjust judgments? Aquinas warns against this tendency: "In judging things we do them no harm, however we judge them; only the quality of our judgment is at stake. But when we judge men, it is their good or harm, honour or dishonour, that is at stake. So we must be biased towards judging well of them unless there is clear evidence to the contrary."[9]

St. Thomas Aquinas: Who Learned Forgiveness Many Times

Thomas was born in either 1224 or 1225 to a noblewoman from Naples, Theodora, who was the second wife of Landulf de Aquino, of southeast Italy. Aquino was the birthplace of the first-century Roman poet Juvenal; the ruins of the ancient city, along with the ruins of Roccasecca castle, where Landulf's branch of the family resided for nearly 250 years before Thomas was born, are still standing today. Theodora and Landulf, a knight, were the parents of four boys and five girls, in addition to Landulf's sons by his first marriage. Thomas, as youngest son, was destined from birth for dedication to the church.

Hagiographers record episodes that seem to confirm God's special plans for him. As a baby, he was taken by his mother and his nurse to the public baths in Naples, where he reached out and grasped a bit of parchment lying on the ground and thrust it into his mouth. When his mother finally got it away from him, she was startled at what it said: *Ave Maria.*[10]

Later, as a toddler, he somewhat miraculously survived a lightning strike on one of the towers of Roccasecca castle that killed his baby sister and some horses stabled below.[11]

When he was five, he was taken to the venerable sixth-century Abbey of Monte Cassino, founded by St. Benedict, the place where most scholars believe the Rule was written. There the child Thomas was dedicated to God as an oblate to be trained in the Benedictine way of life.

This gesture on the part of his parents was not only devout but also ambitious; they hoped that someday he would be made abbot of this important monastery. Years later he was indeed offered the position, which he refused. During his childhood there, the abbey became a pawn in the gradually worsening conflict between the pope and Emperor Frederick II. Upon the emperor's excommunication from the church in 1239, new hostilities broke out between his armies and pontifical troops, and soon imperial forces took over the abbey. Only eight monks were allowed to stay on, which made it impossible for the community to care for its oblates any longer. That spring, young Thomas returned to his family home.

His parents sent him on to the *studium generale* at Naples in the Kingdom of Sicily, sometimes called the first "utilitarian state university" in Europe, which had been established by Frederick as a training ground for future imperial officers. As such, Thomas's new school differed from other universities and colleges of the day, which were invariably sponsored by the church and devoted to producing clerics. Here, among ambitious young imperial trainees, Thomas studied philosophy and the liberal arts for the next five years, and here he received his grounding in civil and canon law.[12]

He was also introduced to Aristotle, whose works on metaphysics and natural philosophy were forbidden, on religious grounds, to Thomas's counterparts at the University of Paris. Unlike France, the thirteenth-century Kingdom of Sicily was a crossroads for Jews, Muslims, and Latin Catholics, and the three cultures mingled easily. Arabic translations of some of Aristotle's previously unknown writings were now available for the first time in Latin, as were works of Arabic astronomy and Greek medicine. From the beginning, Thomas was drawn to the concreteness and common sense of the man the medievals called "the Philosopher." He saw how the genius of Aristotle could help lead people to Christ.

Thomas's education was probably assigned to a master who was held personally responsible for his moral and intellectual development, as was common in the medieval universities. Though little is known about how things were actually run at the studium in Naples, it is likely Thomas was trained in the usual way: through *lectio*, or concentrated study of texts; through disputations, or formal arguments; and through repetitions, or verbal repetitions of the master's words.[13]

This may account for his later belief that the "best way to discover the truth is to have a good argument," a position most philosophers of the day readily understood but one that gave some theologians pause—those who were convinced that applying logic to matters of faith was intellectual hubris.[14]

Somewhere between 1239 and 1244, Thomas came to know and admire the Dominican friars living in Naples. This Order of Friars Preachers, founded in southern France by the Spanish St. Dominic in 1215, was inspired by its founder's exposure to a highly attractive sect called the Albigensians, who had revived the Manichaean heresy so soundly defeated in the fifth century. The Manichees, the powerful sect to which Augustine of Hippo belonged before he became an orthodox Christian, believed that though God is good, his power is limited by the equal power of Satan. More, Satan created the physical world, and God only the spiritual. Thus, the flesh is evil and a prison to be escaped.[15]

Dominic took on the job of reconverting these devout, well-meaning, and committed heretics back to the basic Christian belief in both the goodness of creation and Christ's triumph on the cross over evil. This he did through inspired preaching and a personal commitment to evangelical poverty. The Dominican mandate, initially confirmed by Pope Innocent III and formally approved by

Pope Honorius III a year later, was for "every type of apostolic preaching—the communication of religious truth in the classroom, in writing, in the pulpit and public sermons, and for the salvation of souls generally."[16]

Since preaching had always been the province of the episcopacy, the Dominicans were here breaking new ground. No other order had ever before declared its primary goal to be evangelical preaching.[17] Dominic sent his fledgling friars out to the universities to learn—not so they could become teachers of theology, but so they would be better equipped as preachers.

These friars preachers, like the Franciscans, were also mendicants, brothers who lived in large priories and begged for alms in order to eat. Almost immediately, they became a thorn in the side of the secular clergy. What were they trying to prove with their radical poverty, their preaching in the streets? Were they trying to "show up" the conventional church in some way? When, years later, the clerical masters at the University of Paris went on strike to protest working conditions, their worst fears came true; they were indeed replaced by these now well-educated friars who knew how to live so frugally.[18] The young Thomas was deeply impressed by the devout lifestyle of the Dominicans he met in Naples, and sometime around 1244, when he was about nineteen years old, he decided to join them.[19]

The decision was an unwelcome one for his recently widowed mother. Theodora was counting on Thomas to make a religious profession that would be financially advantageous for the whole family. Certainly, his joining an order of begging friars did not fit into those plans. The Dominicans themselves were concerned about taking in a young nobleman whose family opposed his vocation; they had been through this before and did not want to see another novice abducted by his family. They decided to send Thomas to Paris, where he would be far from home.

His mother heard about the plan and sent a letter to one of Thomas's brothers, Rinaldo, who was serving in the court of the emperor Frederick II. She asked that Thomas be intercepted and "taken by force if necessary" back to the family residence, where his future could be discussed. Rinaldo immediately put together a military escort and went off in search of his errant brother, who was soon captured and taken to an Aquino castle, where Theodora was presumably waiting for him. He was imprisoned in a tower of the castle while everyone tried to convince him to change his mind.

A famous story, not proven but considered probable, claims that one of his brothers slipped a sexually enticing young girl into Thomas's room, hoping to make him break his vows. Instead, "Thomas picked up a burning stick from the fire and drove the girl from his room. Having then made the sign of the cross on the wall with his charred stick, he fell into a deep sleep and two angels came to comfort him, girding him with a cord of angelic purity. The cord was bound so tightly that he awoke from his sleep."[20] In the hagiographic writings, this episode becomes the basis of Thomas's lifelong virginity.

Shortly after this failed seduction attempt, Thomas was taken on to Roccasecca, where his mother kept him for more than a year, trying and failing to talk him out of his Dominican vocation. A sister who argued her mother's case was instead convinced by Thomas to join the Benedictines as a nun. Meanwhile, he used this period of confinement for reading, study, and prayer. After the emperor Frederick II was deposed and the family fortunes reversed, Theodora decided that it was time to let her son follow his chosen path. Thomas rejoined his Dominican brothers and made his way to Paris, then Cologne. Sometime during this period he began his studies with a famous Dominican master and eventual doctor of the church, the German theologian known as Albert the Great.

Albert, who during his lifetime wrote more than forty giant volumes on theology, philosophy, and science, is considered the first scholastic master to recognize and point out the gulf between patristic thought—the perspective of early church fathers such as Basil, Augustine, and Gregory the Great—and the new medieval philosophy, rooted so strongly in Greek and Arabic science.[21] Albert insisted that theology was a separate enterprise from philosophy, thereby reducing the traditional authority of the Fathers in such areas as natural science.

Thomas, Albert's young protégé, agreed with his distinction but believed that Aristotelian philosophy "provided a sound basis for what natural reason could know about truth and thus was a useful 'handmaid' for Christian theology." Yet no matter how helpful philosophy might be, especially that of Aristotle, Thomas firmly believed it could never contradict the revealed truth of religion.[22] He saw that there were two kinds of truths—"those that can be attained by human reason on its own . . . ; and those that surpass any created understanding"—and that the second was by definition superior to the first.[23]

In his forty-nine years, Thomas outshone even his prolific master by producing more than one hundred works.[24] His two great projects, the *Summa Theologiae* and the *Summa Contra Gentiles*, were his attempt to organize the truths of revealed Christianity into a system that was rational by the standards of philosophy. The point? Not to logically "prove" Christianity true, which would indeed be intellectual hubris, but instead to lay out, in good Dominican fashion, all sacred doctrine in such a way that it could be easily and clearly taught—in one case to believers, and in the other to Muslims and Jews in the Spanish mission field.[25]

These enormous treatises, along with his biblical commentaries and disputations, meant that he lived a life of intellectual rather than physical asceticism. He was not "monkish" in the traditional sense; in fact, he was nicknamed "the Dumb Ox" not only because of his size and habitual silence, but also because of his great weight, clearly not the result of extensive fasting.[26]

Instead, he was utterly committed to the intellectual vocation God had handed him—a genuine contemplative—and though he never wrote for his own glory, his two summae ensured his historical status in the medieval landscape on a par with that of Plato and Aristotle in classical Greece.[27]

During his three short decades of teaching and writing, his steadily growing influence inevitably drew him into conflict. When he became a young academic master in Paris, for example, he found himself in the middle of the ongoing crisis over the still-young mendicant orders and took up his pen in defense of the new evangelical spirit sweeping through the church—a spirit exemplified by street preachers such as the Franciscans and Dominicans.[28]

Then he found himself at the heart of the controversy over Aristotle's philosophy and whether or not it belonged in the universities. Later, at the request of Pope Urban IV, he produced several works aimed at achieving understanding and reconciliation between the Greek Orthodox and the Roman Catholics, who had become estranged nearly two hundred years before. His last journey, never completed because he died on the way, was to the Second Council of Lyons, which had been called to promote unity between East and West.[29]

Despite the importance of the issues Aquinas tackled, he never behaved unjustly toward his opponents. Instead, he seemingly bent over backward to find the common ground from which he might present his arguments. Thomist scholar Mary Clark says, "Through his various commentaries Aquinas appears as a student who aims to discuss with rather than to triumph over a deeply respected author.

He therefore seeks to understand the basic principles that structure the author's thought processes. If he finds these principles to be intellectually viable he will ignore many of the conclusions with which he may not agree and stoutly declare himself in fundamental agreement."[30]

However, his natural courtesy did not prevent him from battling manfully when the need arose. Biographer G. K. Chesterton points out that "being himself resolved to argue, to argue honestly, to answer everybody, to deal with everything, [Aquinas] produced books enough to sink a ship or stock a library. . . . Probably he could not have done it at all, if he had not been thinking even when he was not writing; but above all thinking *combatively*. This, in his case, certainly did not mean bitterly or spitefully or uncharitably; but it did mean combatively."[31]

Yet he rarely denounced an opponent and never displayed contempt. Says Chesterton, "His curiously simple character, his lucid but laborious intellect, could not be better summed up than by saying that he did not know how to sneer. . . . He was interested in the souls of all his fellow creatures, but not in classifying the minds of any of them; in a sense it was too personal and in another sense too arrogant for his particular mind and temper."[32]

> *He rarely denounced an opponent and never displayed contempt.*

He was not interested in winning for the sake of winning, only in discovering the truth. Thus he habitually gave others their due in the arena he cared about most: intellectual dispute.

Living Free of Moral Superiority

I set down my reading and hung my head. Thanks to Aquinas, I now saw that my separate but similar crises with Gretchen and Ken had been about more than unforgiven personal wounds. At their deepest centers they had been about truth. And unlike humble Aquinas, I had damned both my sister and my friend for refusing to accept my opinions at face value. The root of my anger toward them was that I was secretly cowed by their intellectual acumen and terrified at the possibility that they might prove me wrong. This hidden fear made me scuttle all the more quickly back to Fort Paula-Is-Right. Safely inside, I obsessed about their motives. For if any disagreement is taken as deliberate contrariness—if no quarter is given for an honest difference of opinion—then arguments are not about ideas at all; they are about character. According to this logic, those who agreed with me were not only right, but they were also good, while those on the other side of the fence . . . well, hmm. Where *were* those exorcists when you needed them?

The bitter accusations I had spouted to Father Isaiah ("She's arrogant! Convinced she's always right!") applied to me more than they'd ever applied to my sister. What I owed her and others was not harmonious consensus—it was natural for people to disagree— but instead intellectual justice: the willingness to look honestly and objectively at the issues themselves. More, I had to learn to respect honest differences when it came to matters of faith. I was the only Catholic in a large Protestant family, and this minority position made me prickly and suspicious during religious discussions. My defensiveness had eventually morphed into "religious exclusivism"—the notion that if people didn't worship in my tent, they weren't really worshipping at all. Aquinas helped me see that when we strive to live in justice, we also protect and honor each person's right to meet God in the privacy of his or her own soul. Indeed, the Catholic *Catechism* is firm about this: "To be human, 'man's response to God by faith must be free, and . . . therefore nobody is to be forced to embrace the faith against his will. The act of faith is of its very nature a free act.'"[33]

I was ashamed of myself, but that in itself was progress of a certain kind. Pieper says, "The just man recognizes when wrong has been done, admits to his own injustice, and endeavors to eradicate it." I'd learned this the hard way, and the lesson was not one I'd forget. Yet what worried me now was that there seemed to be no way to "make right" the damage done to my relationships with two special people, despite my chastened heart. Forgiveness was one thing, but reconciliation was quite another, as Gretchen and I had already discovered in our efforts to rebuild sisterhood. When we treat a friend unjustly, we steal something precious from the friendship that can never be paid back.

Aquinas points out that justice does indeed have its limits. Certain debts—for example, the debt we owe God for creating us, and the debt we owe our parents for producing and raising us—are simply permanent, no matter how hard we work to show our gratitude, no matter what gifts we offer in repayment. These relationships are by their nature unequal; the strict rule of giving each his due cannot apply in these cases. For the just person, this inability to "give back" in some measure what has been received leads to a particular kind of suffering, a sense of uneasy imbalance that cannot be remedied.

The only thing left to do sometimes is to pray that what justice can't repair, love will.

This unease can only be laid to rest through an understanding of the full meaning of Christian justice: "To be willing to watch over peace and harmony among men through the commandments of justice is not enough when charity has not taken firm root among them."[34] If justice is grounded in Christian love, we are able to transcend the strict mathematical formula regarding what each of us owes the other. This realization calmed me; the only thing left to do in this case was pray that what justice couldn't repair, love would.

Though I stopped trying to fix what only God could heal, remorse for the damage done did not go away. Even worse was the worry that I might fall into the injustice trap again. After all, I hadn't changed much on the emotional level, despite my new understanding about justice. I was still a passionate, fiery person, quick to delight in people and things but also quick to judge. How would I prevent myself from unjustly lashing out again?

I decided to begin taking note of every negative judgment I passed as I went about my daily business. Of course it was impossible to catch all of these, but simply focusing on my evaluative machinery for a while provided quite a revelation. I found that I regularly tried and condemned other drivers, for example—those who tailgated, those who puttered along in the fast lane, those who cut me off. Off the freeway it was almost worse: nothing escaped my hawk eye when it came to other people's "failings."

After a few days of observing myself in action, I was so ashamed of my penchant for instantaneous negative judgments that it was natural to try deliberately blocking them. As soon as a nasty thought began to rise—*Oh, wow, would you just look at that*—I interjected a quiet antidote: *There you go again.* This was often enough to halt the process, but if not, I simply begged for help: *O God, come to my assistance. O Lord, make haste to help me.*

Contending with the ingrained habit of thoughtlessly judging everything and everybody was a good start. The next step was to turn a highly skeptical eye toward my ability to judge at all. This is not to say, as some contemporary people do, that making rational judgments is impossible, thanks to interference by unconscious motives. Neither is it saying that *any* judging is essentially unloving. But I had used my evaluative faculties rashly, and until I learned to treat them with the respectful care they required, I was still in danger of being unjust. I could tell that for a long time to come, I would need to automatically doubt each judgment I made, to pray about it, and to subject it to the light of God's truth. Only then could I afford to let it stand. Only then might love enter into the act of judging.

Thomas Aquinas's life ended at the feet of this kind of love, which is really divine love. On December 6, 1273, a mysterious event occurred while he was saying Mass. He had always been profoundly moved by the Eucharist and sometimes became so contemplatively absorbed in it that he had to be shaken back into everyday life by one of his brothers.[35]

But this time, he could not be shaken back; all had changed for him, as he said to his concerned friend Reginald: "Everything I have written seems like straw by comparison to what I have seen and what has been revealed to me."

He never resumed his work, and not long afterward, on his way to the Second Council of Lyons, he fell sick. On his deathbed he requested, to the surprise of some of those present, that the great love poem of the Bible, the passionate Song of Songs, be read out loud to him from beginning to end.[36]

"For love is as strong as death," it declares, "its jealousy unyielding as the grave. It burns like blazing fire, like a mighty flame. Many waters cannot quench love; rivers cannot wash it away. If one were to give all the wealth of his house for love, it would be utterly scorned" (Song of Songs 8:6–7).

HUMILITY

THE ART OF HONEST SELF-APPRAISAL

*And if a person is able he should occupy himself in looking
at Christ who is looking at him, and he should speak, and
petition, and humble himself, and delight in the Lord's
presence, and remember that he is unworthy of being there.*
St. Teresa of Ávila (1515–82)[1]

Several years ago, the oblates who live in our area decided to form
a group. We found that it was easier to live our chosen path—an
odd one by contemporary standards—as a community rather than
individually. This didn't mean that we moved in together, though
some of us now do share housing, but that we consciously began
to nourish the connection between us. We decided to meet every
three months for an entire Saturday, sometimes with a monk and
sometimes not. We would sing the Liturgy of the Hours together,
spend half a day discussing a topic relevant to lay monasticism,
share a meal, and—if we had a monk with us that day—celebrate
Mass. Every so often, we would add a special conference or retreat
to our usual routine and bring in an outside speaker.

We gathered one particular weekend for one of these special
events, an introduction to the Enneagram. Privately, I was dubious.
Wasn't the Enneagram some sort of New Age psychological typing

system? I didn't know much about it, and what I'd read didn't reassure me. For one thing, there seemed to be a plethora of Enneagram experts out there, all writing books. Some of them claimed that the Enneagram was based on ancient Sufi wisdom, not rediscovered until—surprise!—the seventies.

Other experts spent a lot of time describing the "real" universe, the one that most of us are currently unable to see because we are so stuck in our particular "number." This, by the way, was typical Enneagram jargon—"I'm a Five," or "I'm a recovering Four." The real universe, which would presumably be unveiled to us as we began recognizing our own personality patterns, did not, to my mind, bear much resemblance to the Christian worldview. In the Enneagram universe, everything was already perfect—we simply had bad vision. Was this what Christ came to tell us? I didn't think so.

Metaphysics aside, most writers seemed to talk about the nuts-and-bolts Enneagram in much the same terms: as a personality system that describes nine distinct patterns of thinking, emotional response, and behavior. Based on the notion that every one of us feels threatened in some particular way during early personality development, it posits that we grow protectively around that vulnerable part of ourselves. This off-center trajectory leaves us with an "explicit perceptual filter" that determines where we focus most of our energy and attention.[2]

Pretty soon, we cannot act freely because we are so tied to self-protection. Ones, for example, tend to control life through perfectionism. Twos try to control it by earning love. The underlying premise of the Enneagram system is that once we identify our own particular pattern, we can begin to free ourselves from its negative hold on us.

Yadda, yadda, yadda, I thought sourly as I read the assigned book. But I had agreed to attend the workshop—and to be interviewed by Torrey, our Enneagram leader, for a whole hour ahead of time, just like everyone else. It didn't seem like a very oblate-ish thing for the group to be taking up, but really, what harm could it do, especially if people approached it from a Christian perspective?

Newly cognizant of our particular numbers (I was supposedly a Three, a.k.a. "the Performer," though the very thought made me defensive and resentful), we were assembled at Janet's house and waiting expectantly for Torrey to tell us what came next.

What came next turned out to be riveting. Torrey had us take the floor, one by one, in our own number groups and talk about what it was like to live from within our particular pattern. The Sixes talked about their unshakable belief that the world is a dangerous place and people can't be trusted. The Eights talked about their constant awareness of injustice and their urge to protect the weak by acting stronger and tougher than the bad guys. The Sevens admitted to being unable to settle down without getting bored and thus craving constant stimulation. The Fours confessed their need to be special at any cost, their secret penchant for striking clothes, their romantic fantasies. The Fives owned up to their inability to "join in," their sense of needing to hoard what they have, their deep and abiding loneliness. And then Torrey called on the Threes.

There were only two of us, and we were married to each other. Everyone laughed as we walked to the front of the room together. Then Mike's cell phone rang, and he had to go outside to take an important call. I looked at the group and they looked back at me. Torrey asked, "How do you feel about being on stage?" I gulped, grinned, gulped again, and began blinking. Was I going to *cry?* I never cried, or at least not in public. In fact, I couldn't. Crying was a sign of weakness, and I was a strong, together person, the kind of person other people turned to for counsel and support. Public weeping was for those dramatic Fours, not me. I tried to say something but found myself fiercely clearing my throat instead. Torrey waited patiently, a gentle, encouraging smile on his face.

"Well," I finally managed to get out, "it's like this. I have to be on stage quite a bit, what with teaching, doing readings, giving lectures. And every time I have a public appearance coming up, I can't sleep because I'm so anxious. I spend hours and hours preparing ahead of time. It's like I can't take the chance of not being the best. By the time I'm ready to do my thing, I'm totally worn out. I . . . well, I *hate* it, if you want to know the truth. And the irony is that everyone thinks I'm a natural." I glanced desperately at Torrey; surely this was enough?

"Why do you think you work so hard at being the best?" he asked softly.

I felt myself blinking again, then hot tears leaking from the sides of my eyes. Embarrassed, I smeared them away with the palm of my hand, hoping nobody had seen, and concentrated on making my voice come out right. "I honestly can't tell you," I said, most of the quaver ironed out. "Only that I've been this way since I was a tiny kid. Always having to get straight As in school. Always having to win the awards. Sometimes I get sort of obsessive about know-ing how I'm measuring up—it's like I can't rest till I've checked my scores against everyone else's."

Torrey smiled. "I knew a surgeon once who was a Three. He admitted to constantly having to look up the number of opera-tions other people did in a day, just to make sure he was doing more." The group, who had been respectfully silent, now groaned out loud. I grinned balefully at them, blinked hard, and smeared away more tears.

"What do you wish you could do instead?" Torrey asked quietly. "How would you change things if you could?"

Suddenly everything inside me grew hushed and still. I could feel myself listening—but to what? No one had ever put this question to me in quite this way before. Over the years I'd learned to delib-erately sidestep my mindless workaholism. But Torrey's question went far deeper; it required me to visualize for myself a life in which coming out first didn't matter anymore. The stillness went on and on, and I listened as hard as I could. And then I heard it: *Be instead of try.* I felt as though the room were suddenly gravity-free. A sweet vista opened up before me.

I gave the group a dazzled look, then swung around on Torrey. "I'd stop trying so hard to make it all happen and just turn it over to God, I guess."

"Do you think you can do that?"

"Why not?" I said. "Why can't I, if I really want to?"

Torrey smiled. Mike peeked around the door, warily checking the lay of the land. Had he stretched out his cell phone conversation long enough? Were they done with the Threes yet? Everyone laughed again. Torrey told us to take a break. And I headed outdoors into the bright fall morning, skimming on air.

Being instead of Trying

The following afternoon brought the first test of my new resolve to be instead of try: a large book signing at a private home, a wine-and-cheese event with hundreds invited. All for me. And it was raining. *Dear God,* I said internally as Mike parked us in the driveway, *nobody's going to come to this thing and I've done lots of work to get ready for this. Are you trying to tell me something here?*

I listened: nada. There was nothing to do but go inside and see what happened next. Armed with my decision to stop trying to win the blue ribbon with everything I did, I purposely relaxed, breathing deeply and slowly and telling myself I was fine. When that didn't work, I began a desperate mantra: *Please help, please help, please help!*

Nothing changed, except that my breathing got suddenly shallower and faster—the breathing of a tense and anxious person if ever I'd heard it. What was going on? Why couldn't I do this? Hadn't I made up my mind to stop being this way? And prayed for assistance, no less?

Then I started to laugh. I was now trying too hard to stop trying too hard. I'd created another competition for myself, one in which I was still striving to be the best. This was never going to work until I really, truly let go. But how could I?

Then I remembered Peter's words to the early disciples scattered throughout Asia Minor: "Each one should use whatever gift he has received to serve others, faithfully administering God's grace in its various forms. If anyone speaks, he should do it as one speaking the very words of God. If anyone serves, he should do it with the strength God provides, so that in all things God may be praised through Jesus Christ" (1 Peter 4:10–11).

God would indeed help me, but only if I could somehow abandon my self when I stood up to speak. My self was not important—only the words God was trying to speak through me. *So go away, self*, I thought. *Shoo. You're not needed here.* Then, once again, I prayed, this time with deep sincerity: *Let me speak only the words you give me, Lord.*

The resulting talk was a disjointed mess. People looked sympathetic, especially the kindhearted oblates who'd heard me damply confess my secret angst about having to be onstage. There was a smattering of applause and a scraping of chairs as folks stood up and shrugged on their raincoats, no doubt privately wondering why in the world they'd gone out in such weather. Certainly nobody surged forward to pump my hand, as sometimes happened when I was really "on." In fact, it had been a downright mediocre performance, a C minus at best. If this was what I was in for, I thought in a sudden guilty panic, then maybe I would have to rethink my emotional, Enneagram-inspired resolution.

However, I needed that big flop, the way we need the achy shoulders, sore eyeballs, and slight temperature that follow a flu shot if it's going to be effective. I needed the actual experience of public failure, and I needed it often enough that I stopped being terrified by its lurking specter. Other people failed regularly, and I didn't hold it against them. If anything, I felt wistful on their behalf. It was only when *I* failed that the world began to end. Surely, I thought, there's a virtue that helps counteract incipient Threedom?

There was—one of the most venerable virtues in the Christian tradition, particularly of monasticism. It is called humility, and frankly, I'd never been drawn to it.

Giving Up Ambition for Humility

James contrasts humility with the favorite vice of Threes: ambition. "Who is wise and understanding among you?" he asks. "Let him show it by his good life, by deeds done in the humility that comes from wisdom. But if you harbor bitter envy and selfish ambition in your hearts, do not boast about it or deny the truth. Such 'wisdom' does not come down from heaven but is earthly, unspiritual, of the devil. For where you have envy and selfish ambition, there you find disorder and every evil practice" (James 3:13–16).

Though I could honestly say I didn't envy other people, I had spent much of my life chasing after the elusive goal of being the best at whatever I took on. In that sense I'd been extremely ambitious, and often enough the exhausting effort to meet my own unrealistic standards had made me impatient with anything that diverted my attention—for example, the perfectly legitimate needs of others. James is clear about the disorder that comes from focused ambition; it is the opposite of what happens when we are intemperate and lose focus altogether. Ambition makes us fiercely, selfishly single-minded; we can't allow anything in but that which applies to the quest at hand.

What happens when we do give up ambition for humility? We become open to the work of the Holy Spirit within us. Into the empty space once occupied by visions of our own glory, divine wisdom may now quietly enter, bringing with it a myriad of gifts. James says that "the wisdom that comes from heaven is first of all pure; then peace-loving, considerate, submissive, full of mercy and good fruit, impartial and sincere" (James 3:17).

However, the space carved out by humility may instead remain empty for a long time. If we have spent years running on ambition, we may need years of its absence before we can safely begin to fill up with something new. This seemed to explain how I could honestly try to set my self aside at that book talk yet still wind up with nothing worthwhile to say. I may have given up my usual attempt to tightly control a public appearance, but that was only a start. Wisdom was not automatically forthcoming. In that sense, I had given a very honest speech: what you don't know, you can't speak about.

Unless, of course, you are faking it.

A sudden cold wind passed through me. Could it be? Had I been faking it? Had I ever pretended to know more than I did, just to keep from letting down an audience? I peeked in my Enneagram book: sure enough, the mark of the Three is a penchant for the image-preserving lie. The Three is so invested in being number one that he cannot afford to fail. Looking back, I could identify moments when I'd cheated to save face—spoken with authority when I was really on shaky ground. I wondered how much confusion I had caused along the way and what I'd think of someone else who behaved as I had.

I knew what I'd think: I'd be disgusted and appalled. What *was* it that drove my lifetime ambitiousness, even to the point that I sometimes pretended to know what I didn't? Then I remembered: I'd read about it in Evagrius Ponticus and John Cassian. I was afflicted with the old-fashioned sin of vainglory, and the damage it was doing to me went far beyond simple fatigue.

What It Means to Be Vain

Mary Margaret Funk describes vainglory as one of the sneakiest of the vices, hard for even a good spiritual director to detect. Why? Because it is so often the hidden power source behind high-level achievement. It produces people who seem to be outstanding, because they work so hard at looking good while hiding or disguising their faults. Often those who suffer from vainglory become "stars," for this is the vice that (unlike pride) feeds on recognition and honor. As Funk describes it, "I actually perceive myself through what I think others think of me."[3]

Vainglory stems from the secret notion that if we can only elevate the self high enough through hard work and achievement, we will finally be able to earn love; we will finally be worth something in the eyes of God and other people. There is a pathetic quality to this vice. It gives us no rest because we are always engaged in this silent competition with others for preeminence. Only ongoing doses of public acclaim can counteract the unspoken dark conviction that, stripped of our social status, we are nothing.

This need to excel at all costs is so strong that it becomes a particular hazard for committed Christians striving to lead holy lives. If we can't allow ourselves to fail in the spiritual realm, we are in grave danger, for the stakes here are much higher and the temptations far subtler. Everything "good" we do can become tainted with the need to see ourselves as holier than others. When we are operating out of vainglory, we do the right things for the wrong, self-elevating reasons. Funk says that if "I am afflicted with vainglory, I

take to myself what is proper to God, namely glory. . . . This afflic-
tion attacks the spiritual side of serious seekers, afflicts those who
have already demonstrated that they can't be deceived by carnal
vices. Vainglory is a wound of the spiritually proficient. Subtly, ever
so slightly, I twist the truth in order to move toward self instead of
toward God."[4]

Now I understood why the Enneagram workshop, about which
I'd been so scornfully dubious, had caused such an earthquake
inside. The nine Enneagram personality types we'd studied were,
from the Christian perspective, really descriptions of sin patterns—habitual ways in which we focus on and shore up the self.
And the workshop experience had ripped open the veil in regard
to my own self-idolatry, my need for constant adulation. No wonder I'd felt so joyfully airy afterward! For the first time in my life,
and just for a moment, I'd experienced the unbearable lightness of
being as opposed to the heavy, constant burden of the praise-
devouring ego.

> For the first time in my life, and just for a moment, I'd experienced the unbearable lightness of being as opposed to the heavy, constant burden of the praise-devouring ego.

But what now? Aside from
allowing myself to regularly fail
at public appearances (which
would soon put an end to invitations to do them), I could
think of no way to start retrain-
ing myself. The measuring stick
had been with me almost since birth; sometimes I could even see it,
towering over me in the middle of a field, a ladder to the ethereal
regions climbed only by the real achievers in life. Most people, I
was pretty sure, never gave it a thought. But for me, its ominous,
judgmental presence dominated the whole landscape. I couldn't just
wish it away, but somehow I had to learn to live with it in a more
realistic manner. The answer according to Peter and James was

humility, but how to even begin? Sighing, I went off to once again track down Josef Pieper's book on the virtues.

"One of the goods in which man naturally seeks fulfillment of his being is *excellentia*: superiority, pre-eminence, consideration."[5] I looked up from the page, startled. Perhaps the measuring stick was not my own personal cross to bear after all. Perhaps other people felt its judgment just as keenly as I did. What Pieper seemed to be saying here is that this longing to be the best and highest is intrinsic to being human. The virtue that subjects this urge to the moderating effect of reason is actually a specialized form of temperance. Just as temperance maintains internal order in areas such as eating, drinking, having sex, and spending money, the version of temperance we call humility regulates our longing to *succeed*. Humility deals directly with our thoughts about who we are.

Funk says, "The practice of humility is to be neither too high nor too low" in this self-estimation.[6] If we see ourselves as more important than we really are, we are guilty of vainglory; if we see ourselves, who have been created in the image of God, as utterly worthless, we are guilty of dejection. The trick is to gaze in the mirror and name what is truly there. In a sense, we are to look at ourselves contemplatively, for as Aquinas reminds us, "'Contemplation' refers to the actual, simple, looking at the truth."[7] Humility allows us to see ourselves clearly and realistically so that we are not tricked into either self-inflation or self-hatred.

Only when we are humble can we safely follow out our natural urge toward excellence. The two—humility and excellence—are in a sense joined. "Nothing lights the way to a proper understanding of humility more tellingly than this: humility and high-mindedness not only are not mutually exclusive, but actually are neighbors and akin." High-mindedness or excellence is "the striving of the mind toward great things."[8] My urge to be the best I could be was not inherently wrong or sinful—quite the contrary. God made us for himself, and buried deep within this natural longing of ours for higher, better things is the longing for *God*. Our striving for great things can be easily derailed by vainglory or even pride, however, if humility—our estimation of ourselves according to truth—is not there to safeguard us.

Monasticism, which has traditionally acted as a magnet for those wishing to pursue a holy life, has always considered humility a primary virtue—at times, *the* primary virtue. The Rule of St. Benedict, for example, speaks extensively about a twelve-step "ladder of humility" that is to be climbed by each monk during the long process of sanctification. Based on Luke 14:11—"Everyone who exalts himself will be humbled, and he who humbles himself will be exalted"—the Benedictine ladder becomes in and of itself a path to sanctification.

Says monk and scholar Adalbert de Vogüé in regard to this key passage about humility, "The gospel maxim assumes its full force only when we, with Saint Paul, recognize in it the expression of the mystery of Christ himself. Jesus has not only proclaimed it; he has lived it. . . . Thus the verb 'to humble oneself', like the verb 'to love', can express deeply the salvation accomplished in Christ. When it is said that 'Christ loved me and delivered himself for me', it is not useless to add that 'Christ emptied himself, taking the form of a slave.'"[9]

> If we see ourselves as more important than we really are, we are guilty of vainglory; if we see ourselves as utterly worthless, we are guilty of dejection.

Yet Christian humility is not about being a doormat. Christ was never cringing and obsequious; instead, his discourses were marked by "fearless frankness," which Pieper says is the "hallmark of high-mindedness." And "high-mindedness implies an unshakable firmness of hope, an actually challenging assurance, and the

perfect peace of a fearless heart. The high-minded man bows neither to confusion of the soul, nor to any man, nor to fate—but
to God alone." In other words, the truly humble person doesn't
automatically give in, give up, or give deference to another. On
the contrary, a person who is humble *before* God will stand *with*
God, whether to fight for what is right or to challenge what is
wrong. According to Aquinas, "a 'humility' too weak and too narrow to be able to bear the inner tension of cohabitation with high-
mindedness is not true humility."[10]

True humility recognizes our creaturely status and our natural
subjection to our Creator. It is an attitude of the will—the same
attitude that Christ displayed in the garden on the night he was
betrayed. This can help explain why Benedict's ladder of humility,
meant to produce high-minded monks capable of fearless frankness
in regard to the truth, so often mentions the fear of God. The first
step on the ladder, for example, involves finding one's right relationship to God. Benedict says that a man should "always keep the fear
of God before his eyes, avoiding all forgetfulness." He goes on to
remind monks that they are "always beheld from heaven by God,"
to declare that God knows their every thought, to enjoin them to
love not their own wills, to encourage them to bear all afflictions for
his sake, and to suggest that they imagine themselves "already present before the terrible judgment seat."[11]

All this grates against our modern ears. We instinctively resist
the notion of our own subjection to anyone or anything. We are
instead trained to work at building up self-esteem, to aim our highest aspirations at something we call "self-fulfillment." This blessed
state, we think, comes only after we have figured out what we
personally want from life. According to contemporary wisdom,
it doesn't matter what it is we desire as long as we pursue it with
a single-minded passion. Christian humility calls us to rethink
these notions about what constitutes human flourishing. It asks us

instead to imitate Christ in his most critical hours: those that led directly to the cross.

My longtime performance anxiety now made more sense to me. Until I recovered a right relationship with God, the relationship of beloved creature to honored Creator, I would be constantly tempted by vainglory and its nearly irresistible myth: that I could somehow earn my way to love through my own industrious efforts. I would never be genuinely high-minded, only ambition-driven. I would never speak with fearless frankness before a group—and I would never be brave enough to keep silent if I had nothing worthwhile to say. I needed the virtue of humility more than most people. And I needed an exemplar to help me learn it. But who would it be?

Then I sat back in relief. It was obvious. She might have been created expressly for the job: "St. Three" herself, the marvelously gifted Teresa of Ávila. I went to my office and scanned my bookshelves till I found her famous spiritual autobiography, *The Book of Her Life*, which had several times put her in jeopardy with the Inquisition. One of the best-known works ever written on the subject of Christian mysticism, her *Interior Castle*, was sitting right beside it. I settled down in my old easy chair for a good long read.

St. Teresa of Ávila: Who Was Greatly Gifted but Learned Not to Be Vain

Teresa reflects the larger-than-life personality of her native Spain, which at the time of her birth in 1515 had become the greatest power on earth. Dwarfing even the sprawling Roman Empire at its height, the Spanish Empire extended as far as its ships could travel. Thanks to Catholic monarchs Isabella and Ferdinand, the Roman Church in Europe was still a power to be reckoned with, despite the various Protestant movements gaining ground further north. Spain itself was just beginning to experience a great Catholic spiritual revival.[12]

Teresa's grandfather was a *converso*, or Christianized Jew, a merchant from Toledo who, to avoid the possibility of far worse punishment, voluntarily accused himself before the Inquisition of Judaizing, or practicing Jewish rituals. The punishment for most self-accused Jews was the same: they had to march in a weekly procession with all of their family members, wearing the yellow *sambenito* with its bright green cross and tongues of flame.[13] When this public humiliation was finally over, he moved his family, including the son who would become Teresa's father, to Ávila. This son, Alonso, eventually married, had two children, and became a widower within two years of the wedding. His second marriage was to Beatriz de Ahumada, a fourteen-year-old cousin of his first wife. Beatriz herself died at thirty-three after giving birth to ten children, Teresa among them.[14]

During Teresa's childhood, the great religious awakening precipitated by the Spanish Catholic reform spread out across the land. It was not confined to the monasteries; even the common folk were swept up in a new, personal spirituality that concerned itself with the development of an interior life, the practice of mental prayer, and the seeking of mystical experience.[15] New printing presses helped disseminate works on prayer and contemplation written by the Fathers, the Scholastics, the Protestant visionaries, and the humanists led by Erasmus. It was a heady mix, one bound to attract the attention of the Inquisition, and eventually it did.

Meanwhile, the child Teresa was growing up in an unusually intense spiritual environment. At one point, she and one of her nine brothers decided to go to the land of the Moors to have their heads cut off for Christ. When they realized that the obstacles to this journey (primarily their parents) were insurmountable, they vowed instead to become hermits and began trying to build huts out of stone in the family garden.[16] Given the religious milieu of the day, their game was not particularly odd or surprising; one of Teresa's uncles actually was a hermit, a holy man who later had a big influence on her decision to become a nun.

In her *Life*, Teresa speaks much about being influenced by others, both for the good and the bad, and how important it is to expose children to people of excellent character and deep faith when they are still young enough to be shaped by it. She was no doubt thinking of her own experience. Before Teresa's otherwise pious mother died, she secretly introduced her children to the kind of reading her devout husband, Alonso, would have roundly condemned, had he known about it. Not yet twelve, Teresa became enamored of chivalric romances, and they had a major effect on her adolescent development, especially after she lost her mother. She was a striking girl who attracted attention, and—thanks in part to the romances she was devouring—she spent her teenage years preening in front of the mirror and imagining herself a heroine: "I began to dress in finery and to desire to please and look pretty, taking great care of my hands and hair and about perfumes and all the empty things in which one can indulge, and which were many, for I was very vain."[17]

Then she became the confidante of a flighty relative. Teresa always considered this interlude one of grave danger, barely escaped. As she says, "If I should have to give advice, I would tell parents that when their children are this age they ought to be very careful about whom their children associate with. For here lies the root of great evil since our natural bent is toward the worst rather than toward the best." She adds, "It frightens me sometimes to think of the harm a bad companion can do, and if I hadn't experienced it I wouldn't believe it. Especially during adolescence the harm done must be greater. I should like parents to learn from my experience to be very watchful in this matter."[18]

When her older sister, who was in some ways a substitute mother to Teresa, finally married and left home, Alonso acted quickly, sending his attractive young daughter off to a convent school. Here, she rapidly adjusted to a new kind of life, one that she grew to love even more than the one in her father's house. One nun especially helped her: "This good company began to help me get rid of the habits that the bad company had caused and to turn my mind to the desire for eternal things and for some freedom from the antagonism that I felt strongly within myself toward becoming a nun."[19]

Yet "during this time, although I did not neglect my spiritual improvement, the Lord was more determined to prepare me for the state that was better for me." She fell seriously ill and had to leave the convent school and return home. After she had recovered enough, she was allowed to visit her beloved sister. On the way, she stayed for several days with her uncle the holy man, who asked her to read out loud to him from books "about God and the vanity of the world." Though at first she was bored, she soon began to remember what she had once known as a child determined to go to the land of the Moors and offer herself up for God's glory: "the nothingness of all things . . . and how it would soon come to an end." This rediscovery of the serious religious life led her to conclude that the "best and safest state" for her was to be a nun.[20]

Her health, however, was soon again in decline. Back at her father's house, she continued to struggle with her decision to enter a convent, yet when she finally told Alonso that she had made up her mind to become a professed religious, he—not wanting to again let go of his favorite and still-frail daughter—forbade her to do so until after he died. Teresa then went to work on one of her brothers, convincing him to become a friar, and it was this brother who very early one morning accompanied her as she made her escape to the convent she had chosen. She says about this parting from her father: "I remember, clearly and truly, that when I left my father's house I felt that separation so keenly that the feeling will not be greater, I think, when I die. For it seemed that every bone in my body was being sundered."[21]

In her autobiography, she is very frank about the fact that she was entering religious life more out of fear of damnation than any great love of God. She was terrified of the person she could become if left to her own devices. She knew how easily she was led by others, how much she craved flattery and praise, and how naturally she could charm and fool people when she chose. She did not trust her own instincts and believed herself—with some obvious justification—to be dangerously weak.

Yet the moment she took the habit, she was filled with a joy that never left her. She realized, she says, that she had now become free from the bondage of self-absorption and self-indulgence and that this new lightness inspired her to take on any task she was assigned with happy enthusiasm, an attitude that immediately endeared her to her sisters in the convent. From this experience she concluded that the "greater the fear [the soul] starts out with, the greater and more enjoyable will be the reward afterward." Since a certain "fearless frankness" was to become a hallmark of Teresa's character, it seems that she never forgot this early lesson in self-abandonment. "For if one proceeds with detachment for God alone, there is no reason to fear that the effort will turn out bad; for He has the power to accomplish all."[22]

When she again began to suffer from fainting spells and heart pains, her father transferred her from the convent to a place famous for its cures. In residence there for many months, she was nearly killed by the harsh treatments the *curandera* (female healer) administered—daily purges for four weeks that made her vomit uncontrollably—and her health was permanently ruined by the experience. Though Teresa records in some detail the painful physical tribulations she endured during this period, she spends most of her time talking about what she was learning in regard to prayer. Her uncle the holy man had loaned her a book, Francisco de Osuna's *Third Spiritual Alphabet*, that taught the prayers of recollection and quiet. Teresa became completely absorbed in learning how to go inward and listen to God.[23]

Osuna's book on mental prayer was one of many that were circulating in Spain during this time of religious awakening. Other sources of information were the *beatas*, or holy women, and men like her uncle who drew noblemen and peasants alike for spiritual instruction. The *Alumbrados*, or enlightened ones, were a new manifestation of an old tradition of the Italian *iluminismo*, in which the soul and God develop an intimate relationship. They were by now becoming a powerful enough influence on the rest of society that the Inquisition was alarmed. Especially because of the ongoing Protestant revolution in other parts of Europe, the church had begun to fear such individualistic, private forms of devotion as potentially destructive of ecclesial life.

Despite her youth and her suspicious Alumbrado proclivities, Teresa's reputation for unusual holiness was already beginning to spread, even within the church. During her months under the ministrations of the curandera, she befriended the village priest, who confessed to her that he was having a love affair with a local woman—a demanding mistress who made him wear a small copper idol filled with love charms around his neck so that he would never stop thinking of her. Teresa realized that he was in bondage and slowly but surely talked him out of captivity, to the point where he was finally able to remove the idol and hand it over to her; she promptly threw it in the river, and the love spell was broken.[24]

Another example of her precocious holiness was her apparent rising from the dead. Finally back at home with her father and still terribly ill, she desired to make confession. Her father, worried that this would upset her in her fragile state, refused her request.

She promptly fell into a coma-like state that lasted for four days. The people around her were so certain that she was dying that she received the final sacrament, was wrapped in a shroud, and had sealing wax placed over her eyes. In the convent cemetery, they opened a grave for her, keeping a coffin on standby.[25] When she unexpectedly woke up and asked once again to confess, her father quickly agreed. The legend of young Teresa continued to grow, especially when she returned to the convent, still partially paralyzed yet with a greater zeal for prayer than ever.

She herself was constantly aware of her besetting sin, left over from her teenage years and now plaguing her in the more spiritually dangerous arena of monastic life. "I was filled with more vanity than spirituality," she admits, "though my intention was good. . . . In wrongdoing, curiosity, and vanity, I was especially skillful and diligent."[26] She became concerned that she was so corrupt that she should not be engaging in mental prayer at all, that she should confine herself to the vocal prayers said by the community.

> It seemed to me that I was deceiving people since exteriorly I kept up such good appearances. . . . For in my craftiness I strove to be held in esteem, although I did not advertently feign Christianity. In this matter of hypocrisy and vainglory, praise God, I don't recall ever having offended him knowingly, because at the first urgings I felt so much sorrow that the devil ended up with a loss and I with a gain. . . . Rather, I grieved very much over being held in esteem since I knew what was down deep in my heart.[27]

In time, and much against her will, she was drawn back into her old love of socializing and conversation (her convent was not enclosed and often hosted visitors). Her formerly intense life of prayer became

a memory, though she continued to instruct others about meditation and urge them to spend time in solitude and silence—a somewhat hypocritical enterprise, she thought, that made her feel terribly
guilty. Finally, she was made to see by a wise Dominican that she
should return to her former practice, regardless of her concerns
about possible ulterior motives. "For if the friendship . . . with His
Majesty is authentic, there is no reason to fear vainglory." More, if
we can nip spiritual vainglory in
"its first stirrings," we come away
with merit.[28]

*God continued to act within
her in spite of her strong
personality simply because
she gave him time to do so
by meeting him in prayer
each day.*

In the end, it was prayer that
saved Teresa from herself. This
despite the fact that her next
twenty years were spent in a
state of interior civil war: she
could not let go of God or leave
the convent, yet she could not let go of her quest to win the love
and admiration and praise of others either. Once she resumed her
efforts to pray, she did so assiduously, going off to the oratory for
an hour or more each day, regardless of how distracted she might
be or how empty the experience. She confesses that at times all she
could think about was the hour being over and states that it took
actual courage for her to devote this time to God, for it was often
impossible for her to concentrate. She credits this perseverance in
prayer with any growth in virtue that occurred in her over the years.
God continued to act within her in spite of her strong personality
simply because she gave him time to do so by meeting him in prayer
each day.

The effects of this commitment to prayer were numerous. First,
she learned not to ask for what she calls "consolations." Today, we
might think of these as "spiritual highs," states of euphoria or great
peace or supernatural power. She believed that beginners on the path

of contemplative prayer can easily be derailed by their longing for overt signs that God is working within them. As she puts it, "There are many who begin, yet they never reach the end. I believe this is due mainly to a failure to embrace the cross from the beginning; thinking they are doing nothing, they become afflicted."[29] It is dangerous to reach for heights we are not ready to attain, and our best weapon against this kind of spiritual avarice is humility. "Since this edifice [of prayer] is built on humility, the closer one comes to God the more progress there must be in this virtue; and if there is no progress in humility, everything is going to be ruined."[30] She adds, "What the journey which I am referring to demands is a great humility, and it is the lack of this . . . which prevents us from making progress."[31]

Throughout these long years of interior struggle, she also learned not to fear the loss of intellectual sharpness and clarity that so often accompanies the entry into contemplative prayer. "When the intellect ceases to work," she says, beginners "cannot bear it. But it is then perhaps that their will is being strengthened and fortified, although they may not be aware of this." Though this temporary inability to think may be disturbing and even frightening, "we should think that the Lord is not concerned about these inabilities. Even though they seem to us to be faults, they are not."[32]

What God really cares about, she assures us, is not our brilliant thoughts about prayer, but prayer itself. On the other hand, we should not strive to artificially cut off thought. "The intellect ceases to work because God suspends it. . . . Taking it upon oneself to stop and suspend thought is what I mean should not be done; nor should we cease to work with the intellect, because otherwise we would be left like cold simpletons. . . ." When it is God himself who stops us from thinking, we understand more "in the space of a creed than we can understand with all our earthly diligence in many years."[33]

She also learned that the body and the soul are inextricably intertwined and that prayer is directly affected by the state of the body. "The changes in the weather and the rotating of the bodily humours often have the result that without their fault souls cannot do what they desire, but suffer in every way." We should therefore "use discernment to observe when these bodily disorders may be the cause, and not smother the poor soul." If we are sick, we may need to change our schedule of prayer to accommodate the needs of the body. We ignore this at our own peril, for if we willfully force either body or soul to do what it is incapable of doing, prayer suffers.[34]

Sometimes the most loving act is to allow the soul to serve the body—perhaps by going to the country so that the body can enjoy a good long rest. "Experience is a great help in all," she says, "for it teaches what is suitable for us; and God can be served in everything. His yoke is easy, and it is very helpful not to drag the soul along . . . but to lead it gently for the sake of its greater advantage."[35]

Finally, she learned that the devil rubs his hands together over those of us who get serious about prayer and trips us up in numerous ways. We strive to imitate the saints, then become nervous that we are being prideful in seeking to fly so high. Conversely, we try to be humble and not presume God's intentions for us and wind up "advancing at the speed of a hen," or simply not advancing at all.[36]

Learning to Get out of God's Way

We let ourselves be intimidated by our own thoughts, which then drown out the still small voice of God. We get a taste of the serenity and peace that follow prayer, then try to force everyone else into the same routine, regardless of whether or not they are ready. We take on more in the area of teaching than we have virtues to sustain, thereby becoming a source of confusion to the very people we are trying to lead to God.

We assume that our path is the only path and thus become impediments to other honest seekers. We consider ourselves masters before we are out of the beginner stage.[37] All this bespeaks a lack of genuine humility—the ability to see ourselves in the light of truth. "Without complete self-renunciation, the state is very arduous and oppressive, because, as we go along, we are labouring under the burden of our miserable nature, which is like a great load of earth."[38]

Teresa herself followed the path of contemplative prayer to its highest earthly stage—the state she refers to as spiritual marriage. Along the way she experienced what she calls interior recollection, interior quiet and peace, the sleep of the faculties, union of all the faculties, rapture and suspension, transport, the flight of the spirit, holy impulse, and the wound of love. Teresa's famous and sometimes spectacular mystical states are partially responsible for our modern conviction that you have to be a saint to be a contemplative. There seems to be no room in such a picture for a normal person with a normal life, so why even try?

More, we secretly wonder why anyone would *want* to go through some of the experiences she describes in both her *Life* and *The Interior Castle*. At times, in the midst of prayer or conversation, she would suddenly drop to the floor and remain frozen in rapture for hours. On other memorable occasions she felt a divine arrow, wielded by an angel, "thrust into the heart."[39] This somewhat terrifying wound, she records, "causes a severe pain which makes the soul moan; yet, the pain is so delightful the soul would never want it to go away."[40] The Baroque sculptor Bernini captures this particular experience, referred to by the Catholic Church as the "transverberation," in a famous depiction of Teresa now housed in Rome: her head is tilted, her eyes closed, her mouth half open in ecstasy as she prepares her heart to receive the burning tip of the large golden spear.

Such religious passion seems frankly erotic and definitely unseemly to us today—and certainly did to many during her era. Teresa was often mocked by men who saw her as typifying female emotional excess, and she was chastised by confessors who saw the devil at work in her. She was stalked by the Inquisition and suspected of holy high jinks by envious nuns in the convents where she lived.

Yet she was also venerated, even during her lifetime, as a wise and devout Christian with much to teach others. Her giftedness was not limited to prayer; the magnetic attractiveness of her early girlhood never left her, and people continued to be drawn to her and influenced by her in spite of themselves. She was a natural leader, charismatic and compelling, and this magnetism, coupled with her reputation for high mysticism, made her nearly irresistible to those who entered her personal space.

Despite her terrible health, she spent the last fifteen years of her life on the road in service of reforming the Carmelite order and creating as many new foundations as she could. Yet her heavy involvement in worldly affairs never seemed to have a detrimental effect on her life of prayer. She firmly believed that it was union with God that gave her the strength and love to serve others. As she explains, "The will alone is in deep quiet; and the intellect and the memory, on the other hand, are so free that they can tend to business affairs and engage in works of charity."[41]

As far as Teresa was concerned, every Christian is capable of experiencing the profound depths and heights of contemplative prayer. However, the health of the spiritual life depends always and forever upon the virtue of humility. It doesn't matter how spiritually proficient we become; all gifts and special consolations from God, no matter how impressive, must ultimately fall down before humility. No amount of study or knowledge can take its place, for it is our only hedge against insidious vainglory, that soul sickness that would claim for itself what rightly belongs to God. "Believe me," she says, "in the presence of infinite Wisdom, a little study of humility and one act of humility is worth more than all the knowledge of the world. Here there is no demand for reasoning but for knowing what as a matter of fact we are and for placing ourselves (with simplicity) in God's presence."[42]

And this was Teresa of Ávila—quite different from how I had imagined her. I slipped her autobiography back into the bookshelf, alongside the Enneagram book that had so convicted me. I thought that maybe I would remember better, be stronger, if I saw both books in the same place—"St. Three" and her life story beside that harrowing description of my own Performer self—for like her, I was having to learn, over and over, the same implacable lesson: "When pride comes, then comes disgrace, but with humility comes wisdom" (Proverbs 11:2).

Could I ever become humble? It did not seem possible. Yet as Teresa had pointed out to me, God didn't care about my failures, only my determination to keep trying. If I did, he would be faithful to his promise: "I am the resurrection and the life. He who believes in me will live, even though he dies; and whoever lives and believes in me will never die" (John 11:25–26). In the end, I couldn't earn that through my own industrious efforts. All I could do was bow in thanksgiving before the gift.

It was clear to me that humility, this virtue to which I'd never been drawn and for which I had no natural inclination, is key to the Christian life, despite all cultural messages to the contrary. Humility sustains us when we fail according to the world's measuring stick. It also protects us from vainglory when we succeed according to those same standards. It is what gives us the strength to put our focus where it belongs: on God instead of on our public image. Yet aside from praying for assistance, I could not think of any way to begin developing this virtue.

Then I thought about Teresa's method, which was simply to get herself to a monastery. Monasticism, with its focus on a rule for life and on communal living, has traditionally provided the arena for growth in humility. Though I would never be a nun, I *was* an oblate. I had already promised to live, as well as I could, by the Rule of St. Benedict. I decided to start thinking of our home as a little monastery, inhabited by a community of two. Almost immediately, my focus shifted from me and my individual dreams to something larger: a communal enterprise meant to reflect Christ.

That small change in perspective proved to be gigantically important. My marriage vows, already sacramental, took on new significance. I saw that in a sense they were equivalent to monastic vows, for they bound me to a specific community for life. When I looked at things this way, humility was the obvious and natural path to loving spousal and familial relationships.

Things and people that would normally irritate me became secret occasions to learn humility. If I could just look first for the way I fit into the larger picture, I could sometimes avoid caving in to my usual pique at being crossed or inconvenienced. Seeing myself as a *communal* rather than *individual* creature took me right out of the center-stage position I'd occupied for most of my life. In my new, supporting role, there was little occasion for vainglory.

As Paul reminds us, "Do not think of yourself more highly than you ought, but rather think of yourself with sober judgment, in accordance with the measure of faith God has given you" (Romans 12:3). He is describing here the difficult way of humility. If we are willing to accept the sometimes weighty burden of honest self-appraisal that humility requires, however, it can bring us to our knees before "the depth of the riches of the wisdom and knowledge of God" (Romans 11:33). And only then are we ready to undergo the great transformation that is being offered us: the renewal of our minds in Christ.

6

FAITH

THE ART OF BELIEVING IN THINGS UNSEEN

Reflect that in this world nothing but virtue
and devotion can satisfy your soul.
St. Francis de Sales (1567–1622)[1]

The summer solstice was around the corner, but our seasonal fog had not yet appeared. Instead, we were experiencing day after day of clear, brilliant skies. Without any shades on our second-story bedroom window, I could raise my head at first light and survey from my bed what seemed to be a newly birthed world: fresh, clean, and rustling with secret life. It was irresistible, and for many mornings in a row I slipped out of bed, padded downstairs in my pajamas, and pulled on my tennies by the front door. By 5:00 a.m. each day of this lovely and atypical June interlude, I was sitting on the bench at the turtle pond, watching the dawn sky fill with rose-colored light.

Most of the time I was so immersed in the beauty of the moment that I was not thinking much or even praying. Yet prayer ringed the hours that followed like an aura, and I knew God was somehow manifesting himself in those spectacular sunrises I just couldn't miss. But then one morning he said something straight-out, something that made no sense at first: "Your journey is over."

I frowned and sat up, wondering if I'd just been given a premonition of imminent death. But that couldn't be—I felt as healthy as ever. A looming accident, maybe? I shuddered: if that was the case, there wasn't much I could do about it. Yet the "feel" of the message was not ominous but calm and settling, as though a burden I didn't know I was carrying had just been lifted. What could it be?

I sat quietly, hoping for more. Then, slowly, it began to come clear. I *had* been on a journey for the past six years, ever since making a long, round-the-world trip by myself. That pilgrimage—to Greece, Israel, Ukraine, Russia, Kazakhstan, India, and Nepal—had rocked me to the core, and I'd been trying to write about it ever since, without much luck. During my time in Jerusalem, I had experienced something extraordinary in the Holy Sepulchre. For six long years I'd been trying to figure out what had happened to me there.

During those few moments alone in the tomb, I was overwhelmed by the sense of a powerful, loving, invisible presence. The sensation was so strong and lingered for so many hours afterward that I found myself breaking into floods of uncontrollable tears for several days following the event. At first there was no doubt in my mind: for a few minutes I'd been in the presence of Christ. Then I began to second-guess. After all, I was worn out from traveling alone and anxious besides—what if I'd gotten a little hysterical? Maybe, on the other hand, this had been some kind of encounter with a Jungian archetype. Or perhaps, as Aldous Huxley might have conjectured, I'd entered into the psychic presence of millions of pilgrims' thoughts and feelings about the crucifixion and death of Jesus.

The more I tried to analyze the event, the more elaborate grew my theories. In time, I was miles away from my original conviction about the presence of Christ. What I couldn't shake, though, was that sense of overpowering love.

Trying to Name the Unnameable

I didn't know what to call love on this scale. I had certainly never loved this way myself, even when it came to the people I most adored: Mike and our kids. Yet all through the Gospels, Christ enjoins us to love one another as he loves us, and it seemed that one message I could safely take away from my Sepulchre experience was this: I needed to learn how to love people in a much deeper and more profound way. And not just my family or friends, but everyone: I longed for a sense of oneness with the whole world. Yet how could I possibly experience this without some major change in the way I saw other people? It seemed that I needed a shift of vision—a "transfigured vision," as I began calling it in my own mind—and that I needed to find a way to see the world through this lens instead of the narrow, self-centered one I'd been looking through for so many years. Somehow, Christianity as I understood it had not been able to provide this lens for me.

I began to read the writings of the Dalai Lama and works of Taoist philosophy, Sufism, Zen Buddhism. I was not shopping for a new religion, just looking for some assistance in the love department. It was encouraging to hear from the Buddhists that the impediments to loving compassion lay within my power to overcome. What I had to do was stop seeing things and people as separate from myself, a type of consciousness they referred to as "nondual." I was delighted to find that the Hindus talk about nonduality too, calling it *advaita*. Perhaps nonduality was the key to that transfigured vision I'd been seeking. If so, what I needed to do in order to once again experience that overwhelming sense of love I'd gotten in the Sepulchre was to stop drawing distinctions between things. Judging was my problem: I had to let go of my tendency to constantly evaluate the world and pass judgment upon it.

Naturally, in my search for a shortcut to love on a cosmic scale, I was ignoring the fact that none of the great world religions in their true and traditional forms suggest that the path to love is an easy one. Neither had I even begun to plumb the complexities of Hindu and Buddhist teachings on the subject of nonduality. Instead, I blithely picked and chose what sounded promising and gradually created a new sort of spirituality for myself, one that combined the most loving-sounding aspects of Christianity with those of the other world religions.

I took up meditating with gusto. I tried as hard as I could to live in the moment. Most of all, I worked overtime to squeeze Christianity, my professed faith, into this new, attractive, and mostly Paula-created mold. It seemed important that Christianity measure up to the high standards set by ancient Eastern philosophies and religions, especially in regard to love. Why shouldn't it? Christianity might look a little different on the surface from the other great spiritual traditions, but I told myself that this was only "cultural." Really, underneath, all religions were the same, weren't they?

Then, at 5:00 a.m. on a beautiful spring morning, God gave me the word: my journey was over. Not only that, but the long struggle to make Christianity "fit" was done as well.

Despite what Eastern writers had taught me about contemplative experience and technique, these other religions and philosophies were not simply Christianity in disguise. The Christ event was unique and thus impossible to explain within a purely Eastern framework. And much as I hated to admit it, a Christian version of nonduality was difficult, if not impossible, to imagine. At best, "nonduality" might serve as the description of a certain kind of Christian meditative experience, but not as a description of reality. For in the Christian view, God and man never lose their own identities, no matter how closely they are united.

More, evil and good are distinct, and both as real as blood; this is why the Christian life is such a struggle. Deep in my heart, I knew I could never accept a philosophy that characterized evil or suffering as illusory when all things were seen as one. The down-to-earth realism of the Christian view was in part why I had become a believer in the first place.

The Difficulties of Belief

The relief at being done with the search was immediate, but I didn't have long to bask in the sensation before a new worry loomed: what was it going to be like to finally ally myself with traditional, orthodox Christianity? As serious as I was about God, I'd nevertheless been holding out. When it came to Christian doctrine, I was used to privately picking and choosing—taking on what I personally approved of and ignoring what I didn't. Could I handle the whole enchilada, hot sauce included?

For the first time I could feel the sobering impact of Paul's message in Romans: "See, I lay in Zion a stone that causes men to stumble and a rock that makes them fall." (9:33). If you sign up for this journey, he seemed to be warning me, you'd better be ready to crack your shins. For your own attempts to be holy and righteous will be broken against the hard reality of Christ. Moreover, you will not be admired for your faith, but despised. The world is by its very nature opposed to the Christian project.

Christ himself said so: you will be mocked and spit upon and forced to carry your cross. You will not be rewarded for your goodness or loved for your loving-kindness but sneered at for your stubborn belief in this unlikely story. They will even call you a fool. You will often be lonely, for "many are invited, but few are chosen" (Matthew 22:14). You might even lose your family, for the Son of Man came not "to bring peace, but a sword" (Matthew 10:34). You could be required to die a martyr's death like Peter, to "stretch out your hands, and someone else will dress you and lead you where you do not want to go" (John 21:18).

Worse, there's no way around such suffering if you truly wish to follow Christ. For "if the world hates you," he says, "keep in mind that it hated me first. If you belonged to the world, it would love you as its own. As it is, you do not belong to the world, but I have chosen you out of the world. . . . If they persecuted me, they will persecute you also. . . . They will treat you this way because of my name, for they do not know the One who sent me" (John 15:18–21).

Hard words. Suddenly, I felt afraid in a way I'd never been about the ramifications of believing in "mere" and unadorned Christianity. This was far more serious business than I let myself grasp during the long and interesting search for a shortcut to cosmic love. Lots of people are on spiritual searches these days. Seeking is part and parcel of our cultural romanticism; settling into an unshakable faith is most definitely not.

An orthodox faith by its very nature lays down boundaries and draws distinctions. Tolerance is not its primary characteristic, and it scoffs at the notion that change automatically equals progress. Worst of all, it insists on the reality of a supernatural, spiritual realm. Thus, I suddenly realized, an orthodox faith would have no problem with what happened to me in the Holy Sepulchre in Jerusalem, for such phenomena—no matter how ridiculous they sound to the modern ear—have been happening to believers for thousands of years.

I realized then that I was going to need a big virtue to handle this unwelcome reversion to orthodoxy. Then I remembered: Christian belief already *is* a virtue, in and of itself. And it is considered a theological virtue, which means that the *ability* to believe comes to us through grace rather than through our own efforts. Without this divine infusion of mental strength, we are invariably doomed in our own struggle to believe through reasoning and evidence gathering.

Why? Because the definition of belief, whether religious or not, is that we have an "unconditional conviction" of the truth of something, despite our inability to prove it logically or empirically.[2] Belief thus differs from knowledge, though in both cases the conviction of truth is equally firm. For example, an adopted child can have an unshakable belief in his biological mother's love for him, despite her giving him up, but the moment he finally meets her and finds to his joy that she does indeed love him, he moves from a state of believing into one of knowing.[3]

To insist that belief meet the standards of knowledge is self-defeating; we can never move forward in faith if we are holding out for incontrovertible proof. The biblical definition of faith makes this clear: "Faith is being sure of what we hope for and certain of what we do not see" (Hebrews 11:1). Aquinas adds, "Belief *cannot* refer to something that one sees . . . ; and what can be proved likewise does not pertain to belief."[4] In Christian faith, grace gives us the ability to believe, though we ourselves must make the choice to do so.

Yet how can an intellectually responsible person believe unconditionally in something he can't prove for himself? Aquinas says that what believers really have faith in is the testimony of a *witness*. A person we trust has told us a thing is so, and we accept his word as true. We do this all the time when we read history. It is impossible to go back and assess the facts for ourselves; instead we must decide whether we can rely upon a particular historian. This peculiarity of belief—that it requires another person's testimony—supports the notion that faith is an act of the will; we freely choose to believe or not believe what the witness has to say.

Under what circumstances do we choose to believe? First, we decide that the witness himself is trustworthy, despite the fact that we cannot personally confirm the information he has imparted to us. Second, we find that his testimony lines up with our deepest longing as human beings, which is to find and ally ourselves with the good. The witness knows something that is critical to our flourishing. "We believe, not because we see, perceive, deduce something true, but because we desire something good."[5] Third, we choose to commit to a relationship: true belief is not a matter of mere intellectual assent to a proposition but "communion with the eyewitness or knower who says 'it is so.'"[6] Or as John Henry Newman puts it, "We believe because we love."[7]

Through this relationship with the witness, "belief is transmitted to the believer."[8] We begin to participate in his knowledge of the subject, and the more we believe, the more we are able to comprehend. Yet because we have not figured it out for ourselves, we remain mentally "restless," as Aquinas describes it. We long for a direct, confirming experience of our own. But as Christians, we've got a peculiar problem in this regard. We cannot even question our witness. Even he—Christ—is inaccessible to us, except in revelation, miracle, or divine speech.

This presents a particular difficulty for contemporary believers. Somehow, our witness has to be able to communicate with us, yet the modern mind is adamantly opposed to and embarrassed by the notion of divine communication—so much so that if and when it happens to us, we refuse to take it in. I learned this for myself after the Jerusalem experience.

Why do we shut down this way? For, as Pieper points out, we have "an infinitude of hidden, often barely discernible modes of shutting the doors of the mind and heart."[9] No doubt at bottom we fear for our mental health. In the Western world of the twenty-first century, a belief in supernatural revelation equates to lunacy. Being able to explain what has happened to us in scientific rather than religious terms—or, better yet, stopping ourselves from experiencing the divine at all—is our safeguard, we think, against craziness.

C. S. Lewis finds this modern need to circumscribe the actions of the divine both funny and pathetic. If we are going to believe, he says, then we must give up all attempts at reining in God and hold tightly to our hats, for a genuine communiqué from the divine blasts us out of the pilot seat in profoundly disorienting ways. "An 'impersonal God'—well and good. A subjective God of beauty, truth and goodness, inside our own heads—better still. A formless life-force surging through us, a vast power which we can tap—best of all. But God Himself, alive, pulling at the other end of the cord, perhaps approaching at an infinite speed, the hunter, king, husband—that is quite another matter."[10]

In contemporary society, the forces arrayed against faith are nearly overwhelming. Though real faith demands unconditional belief in something we cannot prove, we keep trying to make it "work" intellectually, even if that means dropping or rewriting some of the major propositions of basic Christianity. Or we struggle to live up to worldly standards, though they conflict with our professed beliefs.

Robert Coles speaks about this temptation and the Christian response to it in *The Secular Mind*. He says of Dietrich Bonhoeffer, the Protestant theologian and longtime pacifist who voluntarily returned to Nazi Germany and was subsequently arrested and executed for conspiring to assassinate Hitler: "He refused the choice of exile . . . because his values weren't secular. He did not, in the end, regard himself as a university teacher, as a minister, as a book-writing intellectual, as a cultivated person of many gifts and passions . . . all of which he most certainly was—but rather as a disciple of Jesus Christ."[11]

Coles also speaks about the plight of Catholic Worker cofounder Dorothy Day. Though she lived in Greenwich Village for years, wrote extensively for liberal political journals, and drank the nights away with famous writers and intellectuals, she became suspect the moment she began living as a Christian activist rather than a secular one. Says Day:

> I began to realize that in our secular world there's
> plenty of room for social or cultural criticism, so long
> as it's secular in nature. But I'd crossed the street,
> you could say: I'd gone over to those crazy ones,
> who speak—well, one of my old drinking friends (he
> taught at Columbia) called it "God talk." He said to
> me once: "Dorothy, why do you now need 'God Talk'
> to lay into America for its wrongs? You used to do a
> great job when you were a muckraking reporter, with
> no 'religion sandwiched into your writing.'"[12]

I knew about this baffled reaction to belief—I'd been through it with my colleagues at the university, and it made for a very lonely existence for a while. My response to their rejection was at least understandable: for a long time I tried to make my new belief "measure up" to their contemporary secular values, particularly the value that seemed primary: tolerance. I found myself downplaying certain outdated-sounding moral statements in the Bible and instead emphasizing those that talked about oneness and love.

However, many of the secular values I clung to were not at all incompatible with my Christian faith. Most of them—concern for the poor, belief in the dignity of the individual—are directly derived from gospel truths. The problem was that I wanted to *start* with these values in their stripped-down state, disconnected from the ancient religion that gave them birth, and then see how that same religion measured up against their modern metamorphosis. In essence, I had clung to my secular liberal passport long after I was qualified to hold one. The price for that had been a faith weakened by multiple amputations. In order to preserve my academic integrity, I had let go my belief in the transcendent God, I had tried to obliterate the line between good and evil, and I had allowed myself to be lulled into a metaphoric interpretation of the Christian story.

Clearly, I needed an exemplar, and I thought I knew just the man: St. Francis de Sales, the great sixteenth-century defender of Catholic doctrine against the Protestant spirit of his day—an interesting choice given that I was raised Lutheran. According to my childhood training, there was so much evil and corruption in the fifteenth- and sixteenth-century church that Martin Luther had been sent directly by God to clean things up. I had long wondered what the Reformation looked like from the other side of the fence, and now was my chance to find out.

St. Francis de Sales: Who Restored a Culture to Belief

Francis de Sales, born in 1567, was the oldest of six sons in an aristocratic family in the duchy of Savoy, France. As in the cases of so many other famous saints, his parents had worldly plans for him. His father, François, hoped that his eldest would become a magistrate. At age sixteen, Francis was sent to the College of Clermont, in Paris, where he studied rhetoric and humanities with the Jesuits.[13]

Four years into his course work, he became greatly disturbed by the notion of predestination, which thanks to Calvinism was a major Protestant issue of the day, but one also heavily discussed among various factions of the Catholic Church post–Council of Trent.[14] The doctrine of predestination is rooted in Paul's mysterious passages in Romans regarding the elect: "And we know that in all things God works for the good of those who love him, who have been called according to his purpose. For those God foreknew he also predestined to be conformed to the likeness of his Son, that he might be the firstborn among many brothers. And those he predestined, he also called; those he called, he also justified; those he justified, he also glorified" (8:28–30).

According to the Helvetic Confession, an early summation of Reformed beliefs, this means that "God has from eternity predestinated or freely chosen, of his mere grace, without any respect of men, the saints whom he will save in Christ. God elected us in Christ and for Christ's sake, so that those who are already implanted in Christ by faith are chosen but those out of Christ are rejected."[15] The sensitive nineteen-year-old Francis became convinced that if this interpretation of predestination were true, then he was clearly among those marked by God for damnation. The thought plunged him into the depths of despair, where he remained for six long weeks. His prayer during this time of trial is a poignant indicator of his mental state at that time: "Whatever happens, Lord, may I at least love you in this life if I cannot love you in eternity, since no one can praise you in hell."[16]

One night as he walked home from his classes, he stopped in the church of Saint-Etienne-des-Grès to pray before a statue of Mary. There, still sunk in depression, he read a famous prayer called the Memorare: "Remember, O most compassionate Virgin Mary, that never was it known that anyone who fled to your protection, implored your help, or sought your intercession, was left unaided."[17] Suddenly, the crushing weight of hopelessness began to lift, and almost overnight Francis felt himself return to joyful health. In his own account of the episode, he says that an interior voice assured him that his depression had been strictly for the glory of God's name, "which is not He-who-damns, but Jesus."[18] Francis was so grateful for this seemingly miraculous healing that he made a vow of chastity and consecrated himself to Mary.[19]

Out of this hellish interlude in his life also came a bedrock conviction about human freedom and God's longing to save everyone who would come to him. In regard to the verses in Romans about predestination, Francis came to agree with the Jesuit interpretation: God knows what we will do before we do it, though our choices are free, and predestines us to glory based upon the merit he foresees.[20] He causes us neither to sin nor to do good; those decisions are an essential aspect of our freedom as human beings.

Theological controversies such as the one over predestination were in the very air Francis breathed. By the time he was thirty, France itself had suffered through eight Wars of Religion. The issues were myriad but ultimately centered on whether or not the fifteen-hundred-year-old church would continue as the undivided center and authority of Christian life on earth.

Under attack by the Reformers were key elements of the Catholic faith: first, the sacraments, including the rite of baptism and whether or not it could be administered to someone who was not at the age of reason (in some of the new churches, infant baptism was dropped entirely, as were the sacraments of penance, confirmation, matrimony, extreme unction, and holy orders); second, Tradition, or the transmission of Christian teachings after biblical times (many Protestants rallied around the battle cry of *sola Scriptura*, or "Scripture alone," letting go in the process centuries of Christian practice); and third, ecclesial authority, or the hierarchical structure of bishops, cardinals, and popes who, along with their priestly and administrative duties, had for so long interpreted dense and difficult scriptural passages for the mostly illiterate laity.

The three great Reformers, Martin Luther, John Calvin, and Ulrich Zwingli, to a large degree reflecting the new and exciting Renaissance climate of individualism, each insisted upon the same basic principle: that "the Christian religion established a direct relationship between God and man through the spirit of man, so that man was obligated to live by the knowledge which God granted him and not by the guidance of any human institution."[21]

From the Catholic perspective, at stake was Christianity itself, so laboriously hammered out through centuries of councils and so valorously defended by countless martyrs along the way. What would happen when every man, no matter his level of education or moral training, considered himself an expert in biblical interpretation? What would become of the Body of Christ when the church began to splinter and people declared themselves pastors and bishops without any overarching authority to guide and constrain them? What would become of Christianity itself when each person, no matter how sinful or confused, firmly believed he had the final say in regard to his own state of soul?

> *What would become of Christianity itself when each person, no matter how sinful or confused, firmly believed he had the final say in regard to his own state of soul?*

In the midst of these raging theological battles, Francis found himself in a private struggle with his father, who had announced that he had chosen an heiress of Savoy to be his eldest son's future wife. By now Francis had earned civil and canon law degrees from the University of Padua and clearly had a bright future ahead of him, including a family if he wanted one. Instead, he firmly declared his intention of becoming a priest. His father just as firmly refused to give his consent for ordination. Then the bishop of Geneva, acting on his own, offered the promising young man a job: provost of the chapter of Geneva, a position under the patronage of the pope himself, and the highest office in the diocese. Francis's father bowed to the inevitable, and Francis took holy orders in 1593.[22]

In Annecy, the bishopric seat, the young priest began his work, preaching, teaching, and hearing confessions. In less than a year, he was faced with a major decision. The Chablais region of the Geneva diocese had for nearly sixty years been Calvinist and thus separate from the church. In recent times, the Catholic duke of Savoy had retaken the region. Now the bishop was seeking volunteers to reconvert the Protestants, and Francis felt himself being called. However, the mission was a dangerous one, and his father again objected strongly. "I allowed my son to devote himself to the service of the Church to be a confessor," he declared, "but I cannot give him up to be a martyr."[23]

Once again Francis won out, and he soon set out for Chablais, accompanied by his cousin Louis. In a matter of months, Louis left, his personal funds exhausted, but Francis, convinced that his call from God was real, struggled on alone. Most of the seventy-two thousand residents of the area were Calvinists who had no interest in priests or the Catholic Church; nobody was willing to listen to his homilies, and his extensive travels throughout the region put his life in daily jeopardy.[24] As a concession to the very real threat he faced, he made his headquarters in the fortress of Allinges, and he kept on with his preaching despite occasional physical attacks.

Francis spent the whole first year tramping from village to village, looking for the few Catholics who remained in the area and trying his best to establish friendly relations with the Protestants he met. More often than not, he was greeted with jeers and stones instead. His father, who continued to disapprove of the whole mission, refused to send him any money or supplies, and it was his mother's occasional surreptitious gifts that kept him going. He spent many nights in haylofts and once, to escape wolves, tied himself to the high branch of a tree for the night, where peasants found him the next morning, almost frozen.

On the Feast of Corpus Christi, during a monthlong furlough, he experienced another moment of intense closeness to God, similar to the one that had lifted him out of the hell of depression some years before. Nearly overwhelmed, he prayed, "Hold back, O Lord, this flow of grace. Come not so near me, for I am not strong enough to endure the greatness of Your consoling touch, which forces me to the ground."[25]

Back in the field, he came up with a new plan: he would write leaflets explaining exactly why the Protestant schism was wrongheaded and heretical, despite the sincerity and devotion of some of its great leaders, and in these leaflets he would get down in writing what the locals could not bring themselves to listen to in person. He began passing these out by hand, posting them in public places, and even slipping them beneath the doors of Calvinist houses. These small tracts, which he wrote as a comparatively inexperienced priest less than thirty years old, together became one of the most eloquent defenses of the Catholic faith ever composed.[26]

In a very real sense, he was beginning at the beginning. His reading audience in Chablais was by now several generations away from Catholic teaching. Much of what he had to say they'd never heard before. He began with the notion that the church, according to Jesus in the Gospels, has been given a specific mission from God, an enormous spiritual responsibility not to be taken lightly. He compared the Protestant schism to a divorce: "The office claimed was that of ambassadors of Jesus Christ Our Lord; the affair they undertook was to declare a formal divorce between Our Lord and the ancient Church his Spouse; to arrange and conclude by words of present consent, as lawful procurators, a second and new marriage with this young madam, of better grace, said they, and more seemly than the other."[27]

He pointed out that the split within Christendom amounted to scandal and that Christians are taught by Christ himself that "he who scandalizes another fails in charity towards his neighbour."[28] He called religious warfare, or the "great dissension of wills in the matter of religion," "the principal and sovereign scandal of the world" and urged his fellow Christians to "look in ourselves for the cause of our vices and sins."[29] The time, he said, "is evil; the Gospel of Peace has hard striving to get heard amid so many rumours of war."[30] It is one thing to preach reform, he said, for the church is as subject to individual sinning as the rest of the world and must be held to account for it. But this is not, he insisted, what the Reformers were up to when they declared that the church had been in error for fifteen hundred years and that it was now they alone who spoke with the voice of Christ.

Slowly, he began to break down the wall of resistance against Catholic teaching that had grown so high after Calvin's years of proselytizing. On Christmas Day 1596, the anti-Catholic tide had turned sufficiently that Francis felt it was time to offer the first public Mass in the town of Thonon in over sixty years. The church was empty of furnishings, and he had to make do with a simple wooden altar. Amazingly, there were no protests, so at the beginning of Lent, in the traditional way, he offered ashes to his parishioners. Here, the Protestant outcry was immediate; he was threatened with prison and worse and so had to retreat.

Within three years, however, there were enough practicing Catholics in the region that Francis was able to organize a Forty Hours devotion of the Blessed Sacrament—continual prayer before the consecrated bread and wine. A procession of five hundred people walked eighteen miles down the road to Annemasse, where the devotion was to be held, and was met en route by a second procession, from Annecy. In the end, thirty thousand people participated in the event, and numerous Protestants asked to be baptized and confirmed. Eighteen parishes came back into operation within the following months. Eventually, according to Salesian documents, nearly all of the seventy-two thousand Protestants in the area had returned to Catholicism.[31]

Biographers often attribute at least part of Francis's extraordinary success under such difficult circumstances to his kindhearted, loving character, coupled with a "zeal for souls," which his great friend and fellow saint Jane Frances de Chantal considered his most remarkable quality.[32] Before leaving on his mission, he is reputed to have said, "Love will shake down the walls of Geneva. . . . Everything gives way to love. Love is as strong as death, and to him who loves, nothing is hard."[33]

Centuries later, Pope Paul VI would say of Francis, "He is never violent in dispute, he loves those who err while he corrects errors." Even when Francis was sent by Pope Clement VIII to Geneva to meet with Théodore Bèza, Calvin's successor and the man known as the patriarch of the Reformation, Francis maintained his gentle and respectful stance. "Sir," he said, "I have not come to dispute with you but to talk with you frankly about the most important business that you can have in this world."[34]

Love became Francis's hallmark, and one of his most famous books is called *Treatise on the Love of God*, in which his profound mystical theology is laid bare. In this work, he follows closely in the footsteps of other great contemplative doctors of the church, including Basil, Gregory, Bernard, and Teresa. Nothing he says adds anything new to the long and venerable Christian tradition regarding human nature, our struggle with the passions and appetites, ascetic disciplines, and the practice of the virtues.

What he does introduce is the flavor of the Renaissance, with its deep interest in humanism. As he once wrote to Jane de Chantal, "I am as human as anyone can possibly be." On another occasion he asked, "Haven't I got a human heart and a nature that feels?"[35] His respect for our creaturely aspect and his conviction that God made us the way we are for good reasons led him in his *Treatise on the Love of God* to take a strong stand against classical Stoicism disguised as Christianity.

"A great folly," he says, speaking of those who would seek to free themselves entirely from human emotion and desire, "to wish to be wise with an impossible wisdom." He adds, quoting Augustine, "Amongst us Christians, according to holy Scripture and sound doctrine, the citizens of the sacred city of God, living to God, in the pilgrimage of this world fear, desire, grieve, rejoice."[36] .

Like Augustine, Francis believed that all passions stem from love and that it is what we love that determines whether this love is good or evil.[37] An early stage on the Christian path is learning to love the right things. Even when we love what we should, we cannot transcend the natural limitations of human love unless we are infused by grace. "Divine love is a child of miracle, since man's will cannot conceive it if it be not poured into our hearts by the Holy Ghost."[38]

As for faith, it is our guide and director: it "points the way to the land of promise as a pillar of cloud and of fire."[39] Though reason is as necessary as it ever was, faith far surpasses in its reach anything natural reason can grasp. On the arrival of faith, "the understanding puts off all discourse and arguments, and laying them underneath faith, makes her sit upon them, acknowledging her as Queen, and with great joy cries out: Long live faith!"[40]

While Christian doctrine can hold its own by the standards of reason, the person who acknowledges the soundness of its logic without taking the step of faith does not begin to understand the riches waiting for him. "Pious discourses and arguments, the miracles and other advantages of Christian religion, make it extremely credible and knowable," says Francis, "but faith alone makes it believed and acknowledged, enamouring men with the beauty of its truth, and making them believe the truth of its beauty, by means of the sweetness faith pours into their wills, and the certitude which it gives to their understanding."[41]

The Ultimate Act of Love

The virtues "are in the soul to moderate its movements, and charity [love] as first of all the virtues, governs and tempers them all."[42] Francis agreed with Paul in 1 Corinthians that without love we are nothing, no matter what our gifts. Yet love itself is a wondrously simple and straightforward virtue: it "is no other thing than the movement, effusion and advancement of the heart towards good."[43] As in Pieper's summing up of Aquinas's view of faith—we believe "not because we see, perceive, deduce something true, but because we desire something good"—so also Francis was convinced that there is a necessary link between love and faith.[44]

How does this work? First, before we take one step toward belief, we must feel somehow drawn to the mystery it encompasses, so that "faith includes a beginning of love, which the heart feels toward divine things."[45] Second, faith rests on a free assent of the will; we cannot be compelled to believe—we must choose for ourselves. Yet our will is not arbitrary or whimsical in its choices; it is powered and driven by love, the longing for what is good (though of course it can fasten mistakenly on what is not good). Here, Francis builds on the belief of the ancients that love is the "fundamental principle of all volition and the immanent source of every manifestation of the will."[46] The choice for faith is an act of love.

Third, though at the beginning we know very little about what we are drawn to, by following out this most basic, loving urge of the heart toward faith, we arrive at understanding. "We extremely love the sciences," Francis points out, referencing Aquinas, "even before we fully know them. . . : in the same way, it is the knowledge of God's goodness which makes our will begin to love, but as soon as it is set going, love increases of itself, by the pleasure which the will takes in being united to the sovereign good."[47] Like an upward spiral, the more we love, the more we believe, and thus the more we comprehend.

Eventually, in faith and love, we transcend reason altogether, and our intellect begins to operate in a whole new way: spiritually, in contemplation. Francis contrasts the contemplative state with our usual way of perceiving things: "One may behold the beauty of a rich crown in two ways; either by looking at all its ornaments, and all the precious stones of which it is composed, one after the other; or again, having considered all the particular parts, by beholding all the work of it together in one single and simple view."[48]

"In meditating," he says, "we as it were count the divine perfections which we find in a mystery, but in contemplating, we sum up their total."[49] The contemplative gaze is a holistic one, and one steeped in love. We are in the presence of God, and like human lovers who "are content, sometimes, with being near or within sight of the person they love without speaking to her, and without even distinctly thinking of her," we simply rest in God's nearness.[50]

> There is a great difference between being occupied with God who gives us the contentment, and being busied with the contentment which God gives us.

This contemplative repose is easily disrupted if we become overly aware of ourselves, a special temptation in modern times. People who "voluntarily forsake [the state of contemplative repose] to note their own behaviour within, and to examine whether they are really in content, disquieting themselves to discern whether their tranquility is really tranquil, and their quietude quiet," soon become distracted.[51]

Rather than maintaining their focus on God, they "employ their understanding in reasoning upon the feelings they have; as a bride who should keep her attention on her wedding ring without looking upon the bridegroom who gave it to her. There is a great difference . . . between being occupied with God who gives us the contentment, and being busied with the contentment which God gives us."[52] We must stop studying our emotional reactions as though we were involved in a scientific experiment if we are ever to meet God as he is. Though honest self-awareness is critically important to the spiritual life, contemplation only happens when we learn to set aside self-study in order to lose ourselves in God.

Like Teresa and the other great mystics, Francis saw no difference between professed religious and laypeople when it came to living a contemplative life marked by "holy love." To this end, he wrote a famous book called *Introduction to the Devout Life.* "My purpose," he says in his preface, "is to instruct those who live in town, within families, or at court, and by their state of life are obliged to live an ordinary life as to outward appearances. Frequently, on the pretext of some supposed impossibility, they will not even think of undertaking a devout life."[53] They are misguided, however, for he will show that "just as the mother of pearl fish lives in the sea without taking in a single drop of salt water . . . and just as the firefly passes through flames without burning its wings, so also a strong, resolute soul can live in the world without being infected by any of its moods."[54]

I thought about Dietrich Bonhoeffer, calmly heading back to Germany to face his inevitable death for the simple reason that he was a true disciple of Christ. I thought of Francis himself, freezing all night in a tree, surrounded by the specters of wolves and angry Calvinists. Neither man had allowed the world's capricious opinions to dissuade him from following the pillar of fire and cloud into the Promised Land. Neither had forgotten the biblical promise that even a modicum of faith is all we need: "If you have faith," Christ tells us, "as small as a mustard seed, you can say to this mulberry tree, 'Be uprooted and planted in the sea,' and it will obey you" (Luke 17:6).

I felt sad about the years I'd spent trying to cobble together a belief that I could "live with," a faith that didn't conflict in any way with worldly wisdom. I felt ashamed for allowing myself to be infected in this way by the world's moods. Yet I was a child of my era, an increasingly secular age in which people still cling to the great truths of the gospel while simultaneously denying their divine source. I'd been predisposed to unbelief, and as with all types of unexamined cultural mind-sets, I was blind to this fact until I began to compare my way of thinking with the thinking of ortho-dox Christianity.

Only then did I discover the truth: religious faith is not comforting, as atheists so often accuse, but hard. Hence, its status as a virtue. In order to keep it, we must nourish it and protect it; otherwise, it will be blown away by the chang-ing winds of fashion. More, we must never forget that this vir-tue is a theological one, which means that it comes through grace. Sometimes keeping faith means nothing more than clinging with the desperate need of a trusting child.

Religious faith is not comforting, but hard. Hence, its status as a virtue. In order to keep it, we must nourish it and protect it; otherwise, it will be blown away by the changing winds of fashion.

The beauty of faith is its deep root in love—the very love I'd been so fervently seeking when I set out on my six-year spiritual search, and the love I'd met in person at the Holy Sepulchre in Jerusalem. In that moment, I'd been brought face-to-face with the witness himself, whose testimony undergirds twenty centuries of Christian belief. And I'd found him to be just as described: slow to anger and abounding in love.

7

HOPE

THE ART OF PATIENT WAITING

*When I want to rest my heart, wearied by the
darkness which surrounds it, by the memory of the
luminous country to which I aspire, my torment
redoubles; it seems to me that the darkness,
borrowing the voice of sinners, says mockingly to
me, "You are dreaming about the light."*
St. Thérèse of Lisieux (1873–97)[1]

A long-ago wish had come true: I was finally in England, a place I'd
wanted to visit since I was a fairy-tale-reading child. It was as lovely
as I'd always imagined it would be, with its meandering hedges,
its yellow fields of rape, its Jersey cows and bunchy sheep, its great
silent stone cathedrals. Britain, with all its historical riches—how
easily I could settle down for the rest of my life in a corner of this
ancient landscape!

Mike was puzzled. We'd done a lot of traveling, after all, and
I'd fallen in love with lots of places, but this was different. This,
I kept telling him, felt like home, as though I'd been living in a
dream until now and had finally woken up to my real life, which
was not in California at all, but *here*. Didn't it feel that way to
him too?

He shook his head, baffled, and kept his eyes locked on our lane of the A12. This was perhaps the tenth time I'd mentioned the subject since we'd arrived, and I could tell by the expression on his face that it was no longer cute. Besides, he was bearing the brunt of the responsibility for getting us around in my new favorite place (I couldn't imagine taking the wheel of our minuscule Ford Ka and driving on the left, as he'd been doing for the past two weeks), and I knew his patience was beginning to wear thin. Plus, we were headed for Bath, an ancient town featuring no doubt hundreds of twisting one-way roads named Upper and Lower Frog. We would be lost for hours trying to find our bed-and-breakfast.

As it turned out, our elderly landlady, who had not driven a car for years, had given us directions that tranquilly ignored one-way street signs entirely. Apparently she assumed we'd be strolling in from London on foot. By the time we finally got settled in our room, we were hungry and tense, and I suggested we get down to the old part of town to eat and see what we could see before dark.

We headed down the sidewalk, and soon Mike, lollygagging along, was half a block behind, then two. I stood, impatiently tapping my foot until he caught up, then launched off. In no time he was once again dragging behind. After having to wait a third time for him to catch up, I said irritably, "Are you trying to make some kind of point here? I thought you wanted to see the town."

He gave me a look I couldn't decipher, then sighed. "You walk too fast. Your whole family walks too fast. I can't keep up with you."

Instantly, I flared. "That's not true! You know it's not! You're going slow on purpose!"

"Well, what do you want me to do? You won't take a hint."

"You never said a word!"

"How could I? You roared off ahead before I could get my mouth open. As usual."

"As *usual?*"

"This is nothing new, Paula. You and your family have a lot on your minds. Places to go and people to see. I'm just not as quick as the rest of you."

"Oh, *brother*. Are we going down that road again? Leave my family out of it."

"How can I? We're going to be spending the next week with them. And they'll all be walking too fast."

This silenced me. It was true; we were going to be spending the following week sharing a cottage in Wales with Gretchen and her family, our first lengthy time together since the marathon weekend at Solitude Ridge. Sure, I was a bit apprehensive, and I knew Gretchen was too. The last thing I needed was Mike's old anxiety about my high-energy, voluble family kicking in. Though my family did tend to overwhelm its various in-laws, this seemed like a petty concern at the moment, and far beneath his dignity. No, I couldn't take it seriously. "This is ridiculous," I said. "Let's go eat—we're squabbling because we're starving."

We didn't speak again till we'd found the fish-and-chips shop. Then, possibly to make amends, Mike ordered us each a glass of wine. Before he'd taken three sips, I had mine downed. He glanced at my goblet and raised an eyebrow. "What?" I said.

"Nothing. I'm glad you liked your wine."

The alcohol was doing its work in me. "What's that supposed to mean?" I asked belligerently.

He sighed and looked out the window, as though hoping somebody might come to rescue us. "Listen," he said finally, "it's been a long day. A long couple of weeks. We're both tired—"

"I'm not tired. I love this trip. But I guess you don't, do you? I guess you're wishing we never came, is that it?"

This was a completely different old fight—not my overwhelming family anymore, but money. We were both naturally frugal, but when I got focused on a goal, money became no object, at least in the critical planning stage. Mike had been quite concerned about the scope and length of this six-week trip to the British Isles, a trip that absolutely did not fit within our normal budget. No problem, I'd reassured him blithely—I'll use my next book advance. Which I had, but it didn't matter: both of us were secretly horrified at how expensive everything seemed to be—including the small glass of wine I'd just chugged. Neither of us was used to this sort of gushing monetary outflow. And there were four weeks left to go.

We stared somberly at one another across the fish-and-chips. Four weeks, I could hear him thinking. Four weeks alone with *her*.

Who We Are without God

The fight was over—neither of us had the heart for it—but something inside me felt crushed. This was our twentieth-anniversary vacation, the trip of a lifetime. Had it taken all these years for Mike to realize just how little he really liked me? For it was true, I thought as we trudged silently back to the bed-and-breakfast in the dark, Mike purposely moving briskly and me purposely lagging behind so as to show that all was forgiven and forgotten: I was a profoundly unlikable person, and the only reason he'd stuck it out all this time was that he was good and patient and too kind to tell me the truth. He'd been putting up with me—that was all. I was being borne like a burden, not cherished, as I'd naively believed all these years. Finally the mask had cracked, and I saw the truth. But how could I live with it?

In bed, I smiled damply at him when he asked, concerned, whether we were back to being friends. "Of course," I said. "Don't worry. We were just tired and hungry." I patted his cheek and turned away, hugging the pillow to my chest, hardly breathing till I heard he'd fallen asleep. Then I let the tears come, silent and warm against my ear. I was not loved, I told myself, shocked and sick inside. My true love did not love me after all, did not delight in my presence, as I'd always believed, but bore me year after endless year, a soul-crushing obligation.

It was not his fault he didn't love me—nobody could. I was a bossy, headstrong, self-centered person who rode roughshod over anybody who got in my way. I bulldozed. I squashed. I unjustly accused. I was oblivious, clueless, heedless. Just look at how I'd torn into poor Gretchen, not to mention my old friend Ken . . .

By three in the morning, I'd soaked the pillowcase, but the names were still rising up inside me—all the people in my fifty-three years of living who'd come affectionately into my world at some point, only to make their stealthy escape later. They'd discovered the same truth Mike had discovered, but unlike him, who out of love concealed what he knew, they had gotten out as soon as they could.

At 4:00 a.m. I crawled out of bed and sat on the floor in the dark, trying to stop the terrible downward spiral by praying. *How can I live with this?* I asked God. *What can I do?* Then I grew still. What if God couldn't love me either? In fact, who was I kidding? If Mike, a person I loved to distraction, could barely endure my brassy, selfish behavior, how had God put up with me all these years?

Fear descended, quite different from the old fear of the abyss and nothingness. The answer to my question was right in the Bible. There were some people God spewed out of his mouth. There were some he did not recognize. I began to shiver.

But Mike had his unlikable side too. Sometimes he was pushy and willful; sometimes he got just as snappy as I did. Ditto for Gretchen, Ken, and all the other supposed victims of my horridness. When it came to human relationships, we were *all* guilty. Maybe Sartre was right; maybe hell really was other people. If so, how did we Christians dare hope for a new heaven and a new earth where the lion would lie down with the lamb? Most of us couldn't even get through a dinner-table conversation without offending each other. Where was the transformation? Where was the glory?

Maybe Christianity was just a consoling fantasy after all.

My head, which had been buried in my hands, snapped up. I'd been down this path before, and I knew just what lay at the end of it. And I *wasn't* going there again. *O God, come to my assistance*, I prayed. *O Lord, make haste to help me.*

Moments later, my ragged breathing began to even out. I looked up at the window shade, edged in the faint pink light of dawn. I felt the floor, hard and reassuring beneath my crossed legs. It was going to be okay. He was there. He was listening. He hadn't spewed me out of his mouth. *So, I asked him, what do we do?*

Love one another as I have loved you, he said as the first narrow beam from the rising sun struck the wall in front of me.

I crawled thoughtfully back into bed and put my arms around Mike, who muttered in his sleep and shifted until we were cuddled safely together. In two minutes, I was gone, not waking again till nearly nine.

Later that week, at the cottage in Wales, I confided some of this to Gretchen, who said, "Every so often we have to stand face-to-face with who we are without God."

"That's true," I said, "but it was so painful! I almost gave up on the whole quest."

"That's why hope is a virtue," she said. "You can have all the faith in the world, but it's hope that keeps you moving forward."

A light went on. My sister had put her finger on a grave weakness in my spiritual life. It is one thing to wrestle with doubt about faith—doubt can even serve to keep faith vibrant and free of complacency. It's another thing entirely to believe and yet despair. It was time to learn more about the second of the great theological virtues of faith, hope, and love.

The Virtue between Someday and Not Yet

Hope, according to Aquinas, is what fills the gap in the Christian life between "someday" and "not yet." It points us toward our true home, whose outlines can be faintly discerned in whatever on earth is beautiful, true, and good; yet at the same time it quietly reminds us that we are merely passing through. As Christians, we remain pilgrim people until the moment of death. Even those of us who achieve mystical union with God—even the great contemplatives—remain in this *status viatoris*, or "state of being on the way," until we leave the physical realm behind us.[2]

The pilgrim nature of Christian life is what sets it apart from the religions and philosophies of enlightenment. There is no Christian equivalent to Plato's vision of the sun, despite the mystical heights reached by saints such as Basil, Gregory, Bernard, and Teresa. For as Paul says in 1 Corinthians, "We know in part and we prophesy in part, but when perfection comes, the imperfect disappears. . . . Now we see but a poor reflection as in a mirror; then we shall see face to face. Now I know in part; then I shall know fully, even as I am fully known" (13:9–10, 12).

According to St. Aelred of Rievaulx, we humans are like the prodigal son who has deliberately abandoned his loving father. Like the miserable prodigal, we wander in the "land of unlikeness," seeking the place we truly belong.[3] If we hold on to this faint but radiant vision of our true home and do not give up the quest, "peace, quiet, happiness . . . await us in the homeland of our hope."[4] But not yet. Not in this world.

The magnetic attractiveness of this distant homeland makes our earthly lives an endless pilgrimage, fueled by a "holy longing" for what is to come.[5] "Inside of us, . . . something is at odds with the very rhythm of things," says Ronald Rolheiser, "and we are forever restless, dissatisfied, frustrated, and aching. We are so overcharged with desire that it is hard to come to simple rest."[6]

We are condemned to suffer this otherwise inexplicable restlessness until the moment we fully grasp the implications of the Christian story and its promise of eternal life. G. K. Chesterton speaks of his relief at discovering the true nature of his dissatisfaction: "The modern philosopher had told me again and again that I was in the right place, and I had still felt depressed even in acquiescence. But I had heard that I was in the *wrong* place, and my soul sang for joy, like a bird in spring. The knowledge found out and illuminated forgotten chambers in the dark house of infancy. I knew now why grass had always seemed to me as queer as the green beard of a giant, and why I could feel homesick at home."[7]

Yet we cannot skip this earthly part of the spiritual journey. We must travel through time until, at the moment of death, we step out of temporality and into eternity.[8] And in between we must grapple with the challenge of maintaining forward momentum, despite our unsatisfied longing. To stop, to lose hope, is to sink toward the antithesis of human fulfillment, which is nothingness. The difficult way of the pilgrim, says Pieper, even when it involves great suffering and doubt, leads in exactly the opposite direction—"toward being and away from nothingness; it leads to realization, not to annihilation."[9] The danger that attends the status viatoris is that we are "not yet" safe from the fall into nothingness as long as we are in this earthly life. The virtue of hope saves us from this disastrous end.

> We must grapple with the challenge of maintaining forward momentum, despite our unsatisfied longing.

We are born with a natural hopefulness. When we are young, we hope for love and success. When life becomes difficult, we hope for the best. When we are old, we hope for a good death. Deep within this natural hope of ours lies the aspiration to great things. Also known as magnanimity, this deep-seated urge to achieve is what "decides in favor of what is, at any given moment, the greater possibility of the human potentiality for being."[10] Without natural hope there is no impetus for growth and change; yet too much natural hope can lead to psychological inflation. Humility tempers this inborn impulse to greatness and keeps us focused on the reality of who we are.

> To stop, to lose hope, is to sink toward the antithesis of human fulfillment, which is nothingness.

However, hope becomes something more than a common human urge when it is oriented toward a "fulfillment and a beatitude that are not 'owed' to natural man"—in other words, when hope is focused on our end in God.[11] This is where natural hope is transformed into a virtue. Like faith, the theological virtue of hope is not self-generated; it comes to us through grace, and we can only cling to it. We can understand the nature of this hope and its supernatural goal only through divine revelation via the gospel story.

What we discover here is that "Christ is the actual foundation of hope."[12] Isaiah prophesies of the Messiah who will spring from the root of Jesse that "the Gentiles will hope in him" (see Romans 15:12). Paul urges new Christians to trust in "the God of hope" so that they may "overflow with hope by the power of the Holy Spirit" (Romans 15:13). He reminds them that it is the Christ within who constitutes their "hope of glory" (Colossians 1:27) and uses the same message to reassure the Thessalonians, who are confused about why Christians are continuing to undergo physical death despite the promise of eternal life: "Brothers, we do not want you to be ignorant about those who fall asleep, or to grieve like the rest of men, who have no hope. We believe that Jesus died and rose again and so we believe that God will bring with Jesus those who have fallen asleep in him" (1 Thessalonians 4:13–14).

This hope in the Christ who has conquered death and promises life is the "anchor for the soul" (Hebrews 6:19), giving us the stability to live for God instead of for ourselves. John talks about this critical link between hope and Christian transformation: "Everyone who has this hope in him purifies himself, just as he is pure" (1 John 3:3). Adds the author of Hebrews, "Let us hold unswervingly to the hope we profess, for he who promised is faithful. And let us consider how we may spur one another on toward love and good deeds" (10:23–24). Hope in the "lasting elevation of man's being" thus depends entirely on the incarnation, death, resurrection, and ascension of Christ.[13]

Even during physical life, the theological virtue of hope offers us such a lengthy future that the past seems brief in comparison. We become like young people looking forward with eager eyes, rather than old people bleakly dwelling on lost health and vitality. Says Pieper, "It seems surprising . . . how seldom the enchanting youthfulness of our great saints is noticed; especially of those saints who were active in the world as builders and founders." Hope is a true fountain of youth.[14]

Yet we can lose this anchor for the soul in two ways: through presumption and through despair. In presumption, we become convinced that we have already arrived. The anxiety-producing "not yet" of the pilgrim journey is set aside for the more comforting notion that the trip is over and all is well. We have no more to learn, no more to suffer, and no more changes to undergo; we are now perfected beings and the process is done. Presumption may be the great temptation of the New Age and other philosophies of enlightenment in which the way of knowledge (gnosis) and not the way of Christ is seen as the path to deification.

Presumption also shows up in various forms of Christian triumphalism. Catholics, Evangelicals, Pentecostals, Calvinists, and countless other Christians have throughout the centuries too often embraced the dangerous notion that their particular doctrine and practice are perfect. Christ has no more to teach them; on the contrary, they themselves have been chosen as his personal mouthpieces. For example, Christians who focus almost solely on atonement and salvation can fall into the presumptuous notion that just because they've accepted Christ as their personal savior, their job is done and heaven is assured. On the other hand, Christians who focus on charitable works can be trapped by the presumption that their goodness is all God requires of them. Finally, those who practice the virtues can slip into a presumptuous vision of themselves as perfected creatures. In each of these cases, the sin against hope lies in substituting the "not yet" of the status viatoris with the "already" of life after death.

Despair, the other sin against hope, is an anticipation of nonfulfillment. In despair we do not simply claim that the quest is too difficult; we claim that it is doomed. Despair used in this sense does not refer to the psychological state of discouragement or depression; it is not a mood but a decision of the will. We choose, despite the promises of Christ, to privately believe that the project will never work. This attitude then determines our conduct. Says Pieper, "The despair of which we are speaking is a sin. A sin, moreover, that bears the mark of special gravity and of an intensity of evil." Why? Because for the Christian, "despair is a decision against Christ. It is a denial of the redemption."[15] It is also an anticipation of damnation—the same anticipation Frances de Sales suffered through during those six weeks of believing himself predestined to hell. Finally, despair directly contradicts the basic premise of Christian anthropology: that we are made for God and meant to be super-naturally fulfilled.

The root of despair is acedia, or spiritual sloth. This particular form of sloth, says Mary Margaret Funk, is not about laziness but "weariness of the soul": "I hear in my head the constant refrain, What's the use?"[16] The core thought, unexpressed, is that the quest is ultimately doomed anyway, so why keep at it? This sense that effort is useless becomes an insidious destroyer of the spiritual life as a whole.

I thought back to that long dark night on the floor of the bed-and-breakfast and how quickly the discouragement about my own seemingly intractable sinfulness led me to the threshold of despair. I went back over the steps of my middle-of-the-night argument against hope—both for myself and for the rest of humanity. And I saw how inexorably despair leads to outright denial: in my case, the bitter thought that Christianity might be only a consoling fantasy.

St. Thérèse of Lisieux: Whose Short Life Was a Journey of Suffering—and Hope

Whose story could I read? It had to be someone who had walked through the valley of the shadow and never relinquished hope. It had to be someone who'd truly suffered, with little reward to show for it. Then I remembered Thérèse of Lisieux, who died an ago-nizing death of tuberculosis in a small Carmelite convent at the age of twenty-four. Her religious life was conducted in almost total obscurity, yet within a hundred years of her death she had been not only canonized but also declared a doctor of the church.

Thérèse was born in Alençon, France, on a cold winter night in 1873, the last of nine children of Louis and Zélie Martin. Her par-ents had already lost three infants and a five-year-old, so Thérèse was welcomed by the whole family as a gift.[17] The sisters who stood around the bed of Zélie and the new baby ranged in age from four to nearly thirteen. The oldest, Marie, was declared godmother at the baptism, which took place two days later.[18]

The infant Thérèse soon fell seriously ill, and Zélie despaired of saving her. The family doctor advised that the baby be given over to the care of a wet nurse in the country, where fresh air, sunshine, and a hearty diet might stop the steady decline. Two-month-old Thérèse was sent to live with Rose Taille on a farm eight miles away and remained there for nearly a year. She grew into a big, strong baby, blond and tanned and happy. As her mother wrote some months later, "Her nurse brings her out to the fields in a wheelbarrow, seated on top a load of hay; she hardly ever cries. Little Rose says that one could hardly find a better child."[19]

In time, the toddler was deemed healthy enough to come home, where she was once again welcomed with great joy and thanksgiving. As Thérèse later wrote at the beginning of her famous spiritual autobiography, *The Story of a Soul*, her life was destined to be short but intensely lived from the very start: "God granted me the favor of opening my intelligence at an early age and imprinting childhood recollections so deeply on my memory that it seems the things I'm about to recount happened only yesterday. Jesus in His love willed, perhaps, that I know the matchless Mother He had given me, but whom His hand hastened to crown in heaven."[20]

Zélie also cherished the brief interlude between the birth of her youngest child and her own death, from cancer, when Thérèse was only four. As she wrote to her daughter Pauline, "The little ones [Thérèse and Céline] don't disturb me since both of them are very good; they are very special, and certainly will turn out well. You and Marie will be able to raise them perfectly. Céline never commits the smallest deliberate fault. The little one will be all right too, for she wouldn't tell a lie for all the gold in the world and she has a spirit about her that I have not seen in any of you." Later in the same letter she adds poignantly, "The little one is our whole happiness. She will be good; you can already see the germ of goodness in her. She speaks only about God and wouldn't miss her prayers for anything."[21]

Zélie died in the middle of the night in August 1877. This first experience of loss had a major impact on her most sensitive child. Says Thérèse, "The touching ceremony of the last anointing is . . . deeply impressed on my mind. I can still see the spot where I was by Céline's side. All five of us were lined up according to age, and Papa was there too, sobbing."[22]

After Zélie's death, the sisters drew even closer, particularly Céline and Thérèse, who were nearest each other in the family lineup. On the day of the funeral each of the younger girls selected her own substitute mother, Thérèse choosing Pauline, and Céline designating Marie.

Soon their father decided to move the household from Alençon to Lisieux, where his dead wife's family lived. He thought the girls would be better off living closer to relatives. Thérèse in particular had become extremely shy, sensitive, and tied to her siblings in the months since her mother had died, and she immediately opened up in the presence of her cousins and aunt. But it was the young teenager Pauline who took most of the responsibility for Thérèse's upbringing. "In the morning," wrote Thérèse to her sister years later, "you used to come to me and ask me if I had raised my heart to God, and then you dressed me. While dressing me you spoke about Him and afterward we knelt down and prayed and said our prayers together. The reading lesson came later and the first word I was able to read without help was 'heaven.'"[23]

In the afternoons, the little girl took a walk with her father, visiting a different church each day. "It was in this way that we entered the Carmelite chapel for the first time," recalls Thérèse in her autobiography. "Papa showed me the choir grille and told me there were nuns behind it. I was far from thinking that nine years later I would be in their midst!"[24]

The two of them would often go fishing, though Thérèse preferred to spend the time sitting on the grass alone with her thoughts. "Without knowing what it was to meditate," she says, "my soul was absorbed in real prayer. I listened to distant sounds, the murmuring of wind, etc. At times, the indistinct notes of some military music reached me where I was, filling my heart with a sweet melancholy. Earth then seemed to be a place of exile and I could dream only of heaven."[25]

In time her beloved sisters began to enter the Carmelite convent, the Carmel, as novices—first Pauline, then Marie. The third, Léonie, went to a Visitation convent instead. Thérèse suffered the loss of her substitute mother, Pauline, almost as much as she had the death of Zélie, for a Carmelite profession meant complete withdrawal from the world. Of the day Pauline entered the Carmel, Thérèse says, "I believe if everything crumbled around me, I would have paid no attention whatsoever. I looked up at the beautiful blue skies and was astonished to see the Sun was shining with such brightness when my soul was flooded with sadness!"[26]

Her profound grief led quickly to physical illness. "Believing I was cold, Aunt covered me with blankets and surrounded me with hot water bottles. But nothing was able to stop my shaking, which lasted almost all night." Months later when Pauline took the habit, Thérèse fell ill again, this time nearly unto death. "I can't describe this strange sickness," she says, "but I'm now convinced that it was the work of the devil. For a long time after my cure, however, I believed I had become ill on purpose and this was a *real martyrdom* for my soul."[27] During the many months this sickness lasted, Thérèse suffered many fears, spoke deliriously, fainted, and at times found it impossible to open her eyes. She was tended lovingly by Marie, who had not yet left for the convent.

The illness finally lifted during prayer before a statue of Mary. "All of a sudden the Blessed Virgin appeared beautiful to me, so beautiful that never had I seen anything so attractive; her face was suffused with an ineffable benevolence and tenderness, but what penetrated to the very depths of my soul was the 'ravishing smile of the blessed Virgin.' At that instant, all my pain disappeared, and two large tears glistened on my eyelashes, and flowed down my cheeks silently, but they were tears of unmixed joy."[28]

Marie, who observed the sudden cure, carefully questioned her little sister, who described what had happened to her. Marie then asked for permission to repeat the story at the Carmel, and the next time they went to visit Pauline, Thérèse was interviewed by the nuns. This confused her and convinced her that somehow she had invented the whole thing. Both episodes—the inexplicable sickness and the miraculous interaction with Mary—were to haunt her later when she became a member of the same community. These events seem to have contributed to a profound self-doubt regarding both her fatal illness and her extraordinary spiritual experiences.

Then it was time for Marie to enter the Carmel, and Thérèse went through yet another deep loss. "I was really unbearable because of my extreme touchiness; if I happened to cause anyone I loved some little trouble, even unwittingly, instead of forgetting about it and not crying, which made matters worse, I cried like a Magdalene and then when I began to cheer up, I'd begin to cry again for having cried. All arguments were useless; I was quite unable to correct this terrible fault. I really don't know how I could entertain the thought of entering Carmel when I was still in the swaddling clothes of a child!"[29]

Yet once again God cured her through a miracle. It had long been the habit of the Martin family to hide gifts in the shoes of the youngest child on Christmas Eve. After midnight Christmas Mass in 1886, Thérèse, Céline, and their father returned home, with the thirteen-year-old Thérèse as usual anticipating her presents. "Papa had always loved to see my happiness and listen to my cries of delight as I drew each surprise from the magic shoes."[30] This time, however, he was tired and uncharacteristically irritable. As Thérèse climbed the stairs to put away her hat so that the opening of presents could begin, she overheard him say something in regard to the cherished family custom that pierced her to the soul: "Well, fortunately, this will be the last year!"

Thérèse's normal response would have been a flood of tears. Amazingly, "Thérèse was no longer the same; Jesus had changed her heart!" She recounts what happened next: "Forcing back my tears, I descended the stairs rapidly; controlling the poundings of my heart, I took my slippers and placed them in front of Papa and withdrew all the objects joyfully. . . . Thérèse had discovered once again the strength of soul which she had lost at the age of four and a half, and she was to preserve it forever!"[31]

This little episode became a true turning point. "I felt charity enter my soul, and the need to forget myself and to please others. . . . I experienced a great desire to work for the conversion of sinners, a desire I hadn't felt so intensely before. . . . The cry of Jesus on the Cross sounded continually in my heart: 'I thirst!' These words ignited within me an unknown and very living fire."[32]

Soon she heard about a "great criminal" who was about to be executed. "I wanted at all costs to prevent him from falling into hell, and to attain my purpose I employed every means imaginable." Eventually she discovered her prayers had been answered: "Pranzini had not gone to confession. He had mounted the scaffold and was preparing to place his head in the formidable opening, when suddenly, seized by an inspiration, he turned, took hold of the crucifix the priest was holding out to him and kissed the sacred wounds three times! Then his soul went to receive the merciful sentence of Him who declares that in heaven there will be more joy over one sinner who does penance than over ninety-nine just who have no need of repentance!"[33]

Thérèse had long ago determined she would enter the Carmel like her sisters, but when at fourteen she made her wishes known at the convent, the superior informed her she had to be at least twenty-one to be accepted as a novice. In hopes of receiving a special dispensation, she and her father visited the bishop of Bayeux; this mission also failed. Louis Martin then declared that he would take his youngest on a pilgrimage to Rome to meet with the pope himself if that was what it took. In November 1887, Louis, Céline, and Thérèse took the train to Paris, then on through Europe to Rome.

At the Vatican, while they waited in line for their papal audience, they were told that it was forbidden to speak to the pope, as this would hold up the crowd of pilgrims. Thérèse hesitated, then turned toward Céline for advice, who told her to go ahead and make her petition anyway. She did so. The pope listened carefully, then "lowered his head toward me in such a way that my face almost touched his, and I saw his *eyes, black and deep*, fixed on me and they seemed to penetrate to the depths of my soul. . . . He gazed at me steadily, speaking these words and stressing each syllable: 'Go . . . go . . . *You will enter if God wills it!*'" Two guards touched her politely to make her rise, but she remained in her supplicant's position, her joined hands on the knees of Leo XIII. She was bodily lifted by the guards, and at this moment "the Holy Father placed his hand on my lips, then raised it to bless me."[34] Afterward, she was carried to the door in tears, despite a new feeling of peace in the depths of her heart. By presenting herself at the Vatican, she'd done all she could; the rest was up to God.

Back home, she wrote again to the bishop, who had promised to talk with the Carmel superior on her behalf. Finally she received her answer: she would be accepted as a postulant after Lent. On April 9, 1888, at the age of fifteen, Thérèse entered the once-forbidden enclosure door and found herself, as she says in her autobiography, perfectly at home. "With what deep joy I repeated those words: 'I am here forever and ever!'" Significantly, "this happiness was not passing. . . . I found the religious life to be exactly as I had always imagined it, no sacrifice astonished me."[35]

During one of her first confessions as a postulant, the priest told her, "Thank God for what He has done for you; had He abandoned you, instead of being a little angel, you would have become a little demon." Thérèse "had no difficulty believing it."[36] She knew herself and her weaknesses, and it was during these early months at the Carmel that she began to follow a pattern that eventually evolved into her famous "little way." The first step was to not make excuses when accused, whether justly or unjustly. As the cherished and in some ways coddled baby of the Martin family, Thérèse had never experienced strictness or harsh words. To be wrongly accused, even if it was only in regard to a small broken vase, was agonizing for her, yet she trained herself to accept with humility all rebukes as her due.

Her superior, Mother Marie de Gonzague, required that she kiss the floor when they met in the corridors. Mother Marie announced in front of the entire community that Thérèse had missed a cobweb when she swept the cloister. On one of the days when Thérèse was sent by the novice mistress to weed the garden at 4:30, she was once again noticed by her superior, who commented, "Really, this child does nothing at all! What sort of novice has to take a walk every day?"[37] Over and over, Thérèse faced these humiliations with the determination not to defend herself and with gratitude for the strict formation she was undergoing.

On the eve of her solemn profession, however, she experienced a sudden, profound loss of hope. "In the evening, while making the Way of the Cross after Matins, my vocation appeared to me as a *dream*, a chimera. I found life in Carmel to be very beautiful, but the devil inspired me with the assurance that it wasn't for me and that I was misleading my Superiors by advancing on this way to which I wasn't called. The darkness was so great that I could see and understand one thing only: I didn't have a vocation." Crushed, she confided in her novice mistress, who "completely reassured" her. Still fearful, she went to Mother Marie, who "simply laughed" at her. The profession ceremony went on as planned, and Thérèse found herself "flooded with a river of peace" after all.[38]

Near the end of the following year, a flu epidemic swept through the Carmel, infecting everyone but Thérèse and two other nuns, who then bore the brunt of nursing the sick. One by one, sisters began to die—the oldest first. Says Thérèse:

> My nineteenth birthday was celebrated by a death, and this was soon followed by two other deaths. At this time I was all alone in the sacristy because the first in charge was seriously ill; I was the one who had to prepare for the burials, open the choir grilles for Mass, etc. . . . One morning upon arising I had a presentiment that Sister Magdalene was dead; the dormitory was in darkness, and no one was coming out of the cells. I decided to enter Sister Magdalene's cell since the door was wide open. I saw her fully dressed and lying across her bed. I didn't have the least bit of fear.[39]

She continued to grow spiritually, confiding in her beloved Pauline (now Mother Agnes) that she had always wanted to be a saint but could have easily become discouraged if God had not shown her another path. "I said to myself: God cannot inspire unrealizable desires. I can, then, in spite of my littleness, aspire to holiness. It is impossible for me to grow up, and so I must bear with myself such as I am with all my imperfections. But I want to seek out a means of going to heaven by a little way, a way that is very straight, very short, and totally new."[40] She compares this route to the recently invented elevator and says that her method is for people who cannot possibly climb the ladder of perfection.

The little way is the way of a child ("Let the little children come to me," says Christ). Thérèse maintains that only the very small in spirit can aspire to this particular recourse, for the "elevator which must raise me to heaven is Your arms, O Jesus!"[41] Those who are highly educated or spectacularly good or heroically brave cannot rest so easily in the arms of Christ; theirs is a different path. For Thérèse, God's greatest gift to her was the revelation of her own impotence, which allowed her to naturally and easily rely on his strength rather than her own.[42] "For a long time I have not belonged to myself since I delivered myself totally to Jesus, and He is therefore free to do with me as He pleases."[43]

Shortly after this realization, following Lent "observed in all its rigour," Thérèse coughed up blood for the first time. The assistant infirmarian, Marie of the Trinity, describes the event: "That Good Friday she fasted on bread and water like the rest of us. Besides, she continued to take part in the house-cleaning. When I saw her washing a tiled-floor, looking so pale and worn out, I begged her to let me do her work for her, but she would not hear of it. . . . Then, returning exhausted to her cell, she had another 'coughing up of blood' at bedtime as she had had the night before."[44] Thérèse was but twenty-three, yet this unmistakable sign of a fatal disease flooded her with secret joy. She was going home!

However, she did not yet know what lay ahead of her. The tuberculosis, which would become agonizing before she finally died, was nothing compared to the spiritual darkness that now invaded her life. She speaks of her longing from childhood for a "most beautiful country" not of this earth. But now, "it seems to me that the darkness, borrowing the voice of sinners, says mockingly to me: 'You are dreaming about the light, about a fatherland embalmed in the sweetest perfumes. . . . You believe that one day you will walk out of this fog that surrounds you! Advance, advance; rejoice in death which will give you not what you hope for but a night still more profound, the night of nothingness.'"[45]

The unrelenting darkness went on for months. Thérèse writes, "When I sing of the happiness of heaven, of the eternal possession of God, I feel no joy in this, for I sing simply what I WANT TO BELIEVE."[46] Meanwhile, the disease progressed. For four long weeks, between July 6 and August 5, 1897, she steadily lost blood. On the evening of July 30, she reached a crisis point: "She was suffocating and given ether to help her breathe, but it brought little relief." Believing she would not survive the night, the canon gave her the last rites, and everything was set out in the next room for her burial.[47] But she did not die, and on August 6 her condition unexpectedly stabilized. Nine days later, however, the tuberculosis attacked her left lung (her right was already destroyed). The pain was excruciating, as was the continual sense that she was suffocating.

On August 19, she received communion for the last time. The coughing continued unrelentingly. Then the disease attacked her intestines. Her attendant recorded her words: "People do not know what it is to suffer like this. No! They would have to experience it." Fearing gangrene, her caregivers gave her enema after enema, to no avail. In her extreme state of emaciation, two small bones pierced her skin, and she felt as though she were sitting "on iron spikes." It was at this time that Thérèse advised the people around her not to leave poisonous medicines within a suffering patient's reach: "If I had not the faith, I would have committed suicide without a moment's hesitation."[48]

On August 27, she experienced sudden relief. Her death was still a month away, and during this unexpected respite from severe suffering, she seemed rejuvenated, craving all sorts of food, including a chocolate éclair. As an austere Carmelite, ascetically disciplined and used to a life of voluntary mortification, she was profoundly embarrassed by these overpowering urges for forbidden foods. The community, however, provided whatever she requested, and she ate chicken and artichokes with guilty delight.

The nineteen-day remission ended, and the disease resumed its inexorable progress through her remaining lung. She could hardly breathe any longer and prayed continually to the statue of the Virgin in the infirmary: "I prayed fervently to her! It is sheer agony without any consolation!" According to Sister Marie of the Trinity, at one particularly bad moment "Thérèse cried out in a voice rendered loud and clear by the acuteness of her pain: 'My God, have mercy on me! . . . Mary, help me! . . . My God, how I am suffering! . . . The chalice is full . . . full right up to the brim. . . . I'll never be able to die!"[49]

The temptation to despair was enormous: "The devil is around me, I do not see him, but I feel his presence . . . he torments me, he is holding me, as it were, in an iron grip to prevent me from taking the smallest relief, he increases my pains in order to make me despair . . . And I cannot pray!" Her birth sisters, Sister Marie of the Sacred Heart (Marie) and Mother Agnes (Pauline), both fled the infirmary at different points because they were temporarily unable to bear the agony they were witnessing. Each prayed that their youngest sibling and fellow nun would not fall prey to despair.[50]

At one point, sitting propped up in bed, Thérèse stretched out her arms in the shape of a cross, holding on to the shoulders of her beloved Mother Agnes and another nun. The sister she had known as a mother witnessed her final hours: "I was alone by her side. It was about half past four. Her face changed all of a sudden and I understood it was her last agony. . . . She smiled but did not speak again until just before she died. Her face was flushed, her hands purplish, she was trembling in all her members and her feet were cold as ice."[51]

Then "her breathing suddenly became weaker and more laboured. . . . The infirmary bell was rung and, to allow the nuns to assemble quickly, Mother Marie de Gonzague said in a loud voice: 'Open all the doors.' Hardly had the nuns knelt at her bedside when [Thérèse] pronounced very distinctly her final act of love: 'Oh! I love him . . .' she said, looking at her crucifix. Then a moment later: 'My God . . . I . . . love you!'" Says Mother Agnes, "We thought that was the end, when, suddenly, she raised her eyes, eyes that were full of life and shining with an indescribable happiness 'surpassing all her hopes.'" The ecstasy lasted "for the space of a Credo," and then Thérèse closed her eyes and turned her head to the right and died. As the nuns prepared her body for burial, the luminous smile remained: "We thought she was only asleep and having a happy dream." She was buried five days later on a hill overlooking Lisieux. Thérèse had finally arrived in the homeland of her hope.[52]

The Choice That Is Hope

After I read this story, it was tempting to dismiss my own dark night of near-despair as inconsequential, yet I knew it could not be dismissed. It does not matter how we lose hope; the result is the same. Oddly enough, our best guard against doing so is what the Old Testament refers to as "fear of the Lord." This does not mean we fear God with a slave's cringing fear of punishment; instead, we fear the very real possibility, present up until the moment of death, that we will indeed make the turn away from God and toward nothingness.

The Bible calls this kind of fear "the beginning of wisdom" because it connects us to the reality of our situation as creatures faced with a life-determining choice. Says Pieper, "There is only one possible way in which man's natural anxiety in the face of nothingness can penetrate his intellectual and psychic life *without* immediately destroying it. This one way is the perfecting of natural anxiety by the fear of the Lord." Thérèse's monumental but nearly silent struggle with impending despair in the face of overwhelming physical agony provides an example: what she feared more than pain and death itself was letting go of God.[53]

Ultimately, hope is not an emotion or a mood; it is a choice. We choose in the face of terrible discouragement to reject nothingness and to struggle on toward *being*, our life in God. It has ever been so. As Moses once announced to the ancient Hebrews, "This day I call heaven and earth as witnesses against you that I have set before you life and death, blessings and curses. Now choose life, so that you and your children may live and that you may love the LORD your God, listen to his voice, and hold fast to him. For the LORD is your life." (Deuteronomy 30:19–20).

Choosing to hope means choosing to live. When we hope, our lives begin to partake of eternity. No longer confined in our vision by the temporal span of physical existence, we joyfully await the new heaven and new earth that have been promised to us (Revelation 21:1). We look toward the future with eager eyes, assured that God will someday make his dwelling place with us. When this day finally comes, "there will be no more death or mourning or crying or pain, for the old order of things [will have] passed away" (Revelation 21:4).

> *Choosing to hope means choosing to live. When we hope, our lives begin to partake of eternity.*

8

CHARITY

THE ART OF LOVING THE ENEMY

*For the Christian there is no "strange human being." He
is in every instance the "neighbor" whom we have with
us and who is most in need of us. It makes no difference
whether he is related or not, whether we "like" him or
not, whether he is "morally worthy" of help or not. The
love of Christ knows no bounds, it never ceases, it never
withdraws in the face of hatred or foul play.*

Edith Stein, St. Teresa Benedicta of the Cross (1891–1942)[1]

Our time with Gretchen's family in Wales was over, and we had
joined our pilgrimage group in London—a collection of Camaldolese
oblates and a monk, plus Episcopalian priests, spiritual directors,
and teachers—for a two-week journey through the great Christian
sites of England. Our leader, Deborah Smith Douglas, was the
coauthor, with her husband, of an intriguing book, *Pilgrims in the
Kingdom*. An American, she and her husband, David, had lived in
Scotland with their children for several years, and the two authors
had traveled individually to numerous places of pilgrimage in the
British Isles.

Now we were in Canterbury, standing before the eight-hundred-
year-old shrine of St. Thomas Becket. For a place known for

miracles, the shrine was surprisingly simple: a single candle burning in the center of the cathedral floor. Centuries of pilgrims' knees had worn deep hollows in the stone steps. Deborah said, "There's a long tradition here at Canterbury that you leave a gift or offering on the altar when you depart. Maybe each of us could think of something we'd like to symbolically give up to this place."

That night I leaned against the broad window ledge of our room at the International Study Center, sipping my wine and gazing out at the massive, floodlit cathedral, the "current" version of a church that has stood on this site since the early seventh century. Somewhere deep inside the great Gothic structure, an organist was practicing a haunting Toccata and Fugue. The darkness vibrated under Bach's pounding chords. I wondered what my offering would be. I didn't know yet, only that it had to be something that surprised me with its profound rightness.

Three days later, the pilgrimage moved north, with my offering still unmade. We visited York, Durham, Ely, Ampleforth, Rievaulx, and Fountains without anything occurring to me. But then, on Holy Island, Lindisfarne, I came upon a startling, life-sized statue in the chapel—six monks bearing a coffin on their shoulders: that of the seventh-century St. Cuthbert, being spirited away during the Viking invasions of the 800s. I knew that his determined-looking pallbearers were fated to grow old and die before their quest was over; the body of St. Cuthbert would be handed down through several generations of shrine bearers before it came to its final rest in 1104 in the newly completed east end of Durham Cathedral.[2]

Finding the Needy, Resentful Child Within

Thanks, perhaps, to Cuthbert, that night on Holy Island I had a compelling dream. I was startled awake by the image of a small towhead with pigtails, squinting at me through narrow blue eyes.

Distressed by her challenging glare, I tried to think who this strange child might be. And then I knew. I'd been dreaming about myself, the unappealing creature who'd spent so many years trapped by impotent rage. I'd been dreaming about myself in my most repugnant form—that of the needy, resentful child.

This was a version of me I'd long since rejected. For years, I'd avoided looking at photographs taken of me before adolescence. Whenever I thought of those unhappy days, I shuddered. I'd regularly punched my younger brother Ron, sassed my mother, barred little Gretchen from my bedroom. I'd also stolen gum from my sister Gail, refused to do household chores, and buried loathsome vegetables from my dinner plate in the backyard. Whenever I looked in the mirror during those years, I was filled with helpless horror. Why was I so friendless and ugly when Gail and Gretchen were so beautiful and sweet?

When the long transition from awkward duckling to respectable swan had finally been made, I wanted nothing more to do with that old version of myself—ever. But here on Holy Island, this horrid little girl I'd refused to think about for years had somehow been resurrected, and I couldn't figure out why.

Then I understood. I'd finally been shown what I should leave behind on the Canterbury altar. It was time to offer this ugly duckling—a creature who had never really existed, except in my undeveloped and exaggerated childish imagination—into the hands of God. This hateful image of myself had been a millstone around my neck for years, affecting my whole trajectory in life (the overwhelming drive of a Three to prove herself the best, for example), and had filled me with secret and destructive self-doubt (who could ever *really* love me?). I had to let her go.

But how could I let go of an image I had held so long that it was a deeply ingrained emotional habit? I thought then of the long night in

Bath and the trenchant phrase, caught in the air, that had finally put an end to the struggle: *Love one another as I have loved you.* In these words I'd discovered the only possible antidote to human imperfection and sin, and it had saved me from despair. Quite simply, I'd come to see that Christian love is *unjust* love—or, more accurately, Christian love extends itself far beyond the dictates of justice. We cannot possibly "earn" love on our own—we are bound to slip into selfishness or petulance or anger, even with those we most adore. When we do, there is no repairing the situation; we can only hope that those who love us will continue to do so, despite what we actually deserve.

> We cannot possibly "earn" love on our own—we are bound to slip into selfishness or petulance or anger, even with those we most adore.

Now I saw why years of trying to push away this awful image of my little-girl self had not worked. No matter how I tried to rationalize her out of existence, she was always with me, clinging with all her strength and thus blocking my way forward. For nearly five decades, she'd stubbornly refused to let go until I gave her what she had to have: love. If I could not finally, truly love her, I was sentenced to carry her on my back until I died.

I took a deep breath, then mentally scooped her rigid, anger-filled body into my arms. I held her against me, stroking her shoulders for a long time, the way I'd once comforted my own children when they were terrorized by bad dreams. Finally, I kissed her and whispered into her little ear: "I love you, don't worry, I love you—but it's time for you to be with God now." Then I carried her tenderly and carefully to the high altar of Canterbury and set her there, praying that God would care for her from now on. When I turned and walked away through the shadows of the great cathedral, I knew I wouldn't be seeing her again.

Back home, I told Father Isaiah about the night in Bath and what God had said to me there, and also about offering up my child self. "So I think," I concluded earnestly, "that I finally understand what Jesus meant in John when he told them to love each other as he had loved them. He meant we are supposed to love other people way more than simple justice would require, didn't he?"

This was probably not big news for a longtime monk like Isaiah, but he cocked his head as though giving the matter careful thought. "Hmm-*hmm*," he offered finally; then, almost casually, so as not to frighten me off, he asked: "Just curious: what do you think the other version means?"

"Other version?"

"The one that tells you to love your neighbor as yourself."

I looked at him blankly. Quite honestly, I'd never paid much attention to this most famous commandment of Christ. After all, loving people as much as I loved myself netted me a pretty thin version of love. But Isaiah had gotten me thinking. What *did* it mean to love oneself? And how did you do it?

The Virtue That Brings Together All the Others

According to Josef Pieper, love at its most basic level "signifies much the same as approval." Loving something or someone means finding it good. But even basic love goes much further than this neutral-sounding affirmation would imply; love "testifies to being in agreement, assenting, consenting, applauding, affirming, praising, glorifying and hailing." Thus, love is not simply an approving intellectual stance toward something but a passionate "expression of the *will*."[3]

How so? As Aquinas points out, there are two forms of exerting the will. One is a will to action. It spurs us to seek out or accomplish that which is still missing or undone. The second, however, is a "purely affirmative assent to what already is." It does not push forward into the future but warmly and wholeheartedly embraces what is right before us. It says, "I want you (or it) to exist!"[4]

Why is this kind of affirmation so important to us? First, and quite mysteriously, love seems to be the spiritual fuel on which we run. We can only go so far as isolated monads who never bump up against one another. We are made in the image of God, who is—equally mysteriously—three persons in such loving, constant communion that they are One. Baptism opens the door of our hearts to this Trinitarian dance of life with Father, Son, and Holy Spirit, but also with our fellow human beings. As Christ explains, "I am the vine; you are the branches" (John 15:5). Furthermore, "no branch can bear fruit by itself" (John 15:4). As members of the Body of Christ, we are deeply interconnected, and the love we extend to one another is what brings this web of light into blazing visibility.

Second, human love even in its weakest form is rooted in and extends the life-sustaining approval of God for his creatures. For as the constant refrain in the Genesis creation story states, God looked around with delight at all he had made—including man and woman—and "saw that it was good" (Genesis 1:10). Our love for life and one another keeps things going; it blesses the world. By joyfully affirming the existence of our fellow human beings, we mirror God's love to those who still live in the darkness, thereby helping to confer meaning on existence itself. For it is not enough to simply live; we have to know that our lives are worth something. The fact that we can love and be loved by one another is the proof that they are.

This is why people who are genuinely loved seem radiant, brave, and expansive. And conversely, this is why children who are not loved fail to thrive.[5] Love provides both the milk and the honey: the milk meets basic survival needs, and the honey confers the "sweetness of life and the happiness of existing." We feel at home in the

world, meant to be, only when
we are "being confirmed" by
love.[6] Yet as I had already figured out that night in Bath, "at
bottom all love is undeserved.
We can neither earn it nor promote it; it is always pure gift."[7]

*This is why people who
are genuinely loved
seem radiant, brave, and
expansive. And conversely,
this is why children who are
not loved fail to thrive.*

The undeserved quality of
love, when it really sinks in, is almost bound to take us aback. We'd
rather think of love as a reward for personal attributes we are proud
of: good character, achievement and intellect, scintillating wit. It is
nearly insulting that love steps right over the top of these impressive
credentials and gives us what we don't deserve. Nietzsche, in fact, once
pointed out that this is the reason people who are "addicted to honor"
resist being loved. Love does not care a whit about eminence.[8]

Undeserved love also brings with it the possibility of being
shamed. From the great chasm that lies between what we are and
what those who love us *think* we are rises up a fruitful and challenging embarrassment, especially when it is they who glimpse our true
calling long before we ourselves can see it. The German philosopher Nicolai Hartmann says that someone who is loved this way
is "pushed beyond himself."[9] In this sense, love becomes a clarion
call to transformation—the transformation of human nature made
possible through the sacrifice of Christ.

This aspect of love—that it urges us to be better than we are, to
grow into what God intended us to be—explains how the person
who loves us most can also be our best critic. It is because he or she
wants our life to be truly good. Thus, the true lover *forgives* rather
than *excuses* our human failings. The distinction is an important
one. In excusing, he pretends that something bad did not happen
after all. In forgiving, he affirms that it did indeed happen and that
he hopes and prays we will come to recognize this fact and repent.

Love, by demanding the best from us, aims us toward our full potential as created beings, and thus toward paradise. Without it, we struggle in the jungle instead. Yet in contemporary society, the focus is on independence, self-reliance, and getting and keeping power. Our God-given yearning to be loved is therefore often misread as weak neediness, even neurosis. Though at times the built-in human requirement for love can indeed slip into neurotic "infantilism" or the need for "constant confirmation," the alternative is just as bad: "the ideal of tight-lipped self-sufficiency, that gloomy resolve to take nothing as a gift."[10]

Walking this line when it comes to natural love, or eros, is hard enough. Loving in more than a natural way—Christian agape—often seems an impossibly tall order. Paul describes agape thus: "Love is patient, love is kind. It does not envy, it does not boast, it is not proud. It is not rude, it is not self-seeking, it is not easily angered, it keeps no record of wrongs. Love does not delight in evil but rejoices with the truth. It always protects, always trusts, always hopes, always perseveres" (1 Corinthians 13:4–7).

The gulf between our normal, messy, and often-traumatic adventures in human loving and the lofty sort of love described here seems uncrossable, and some theologians throughout the centuries have been convinced that the two kinds of love—needy, desiring eros and tranquil, selfless agape—have nothing to do with each another. For Christian thinkers like Martin Luther, Karl Barth, and Anders Nygren, agape is entirely different from eros and cannot be rooted in human desire. Indeed, they believe that in agape our human personality is transcended entirely and we become only "the conduit, the channel that conducts God's love."[11]

Yet the intellectual giants of the early and medieval church, including Augustine, Bernard, and Aquinas, see agape differently. They believe we arrive at this highest form of love only by climbing a ladder whose legs are firmly planted in eros. Our longing for what we do not yet possess—union with God—is what keeps us climbing, and agape flowers when eros is finally transformed during the purifying ascent (or as Augustine so famously put it, "Our hearts are restless till they rest in thee"). Plato was the first to make use of this model, sometimes called "the ladder of love," which was subsequently adopted and modified by early Christianity.

It is often enough our first confused and fumbling experience of eros that breaks the shell of our self-centeredness. Suddenly, we are focused more intensely on another than on ourselves, and this moment of self-transcendence, no matter how temporary, can awaken our "holy longing" for more. Eros, infused by grace, can then begin to move us closer to agape and our final union with God. In this traditional view of Christian love at its highest, we neither lose our sense of self in becoming a "conduit" nor ever entirely escape the sense of neediness that comes with our creaturely status.[12] And thus loving can be described as a struggle that requires both virtuous strength and the humility to open ourselves to grace.

But the struggle of love also confers meaning on our existence and gives us a reason to rejoice in being alive. Because of the human neediness we can never quite transcend, obtaining what we reach for in love makes us happy. Or, as Pieper puts it, "all love has joy as its natural fruit." Moreover, "all human happiness . . . is fundamentally *the happiness of love*, whether its name is eros or *caritas* or agape, and whether it is directed toward a friend, a sweetheart, a son, a neighbor, or God himself."[13] And thus, "one who loves nothing and no one cannot rejoice, no matter how desperately he wishes to."[14] Father Zossima, the saintly Orthodox monk in Dostoyevsky's novel *The Brothers Karamazov*, puts it a different way: "'What is hell?' I maintain that it is the suffering of being unable to love."[15]

If loving and being loved by our fellow humans and God is the key to a joyful and fulfilled existence, then all love—even tranquil, selfless agape—has a deep and mysterious root in *self*-love. As created beings who are not in charge of our own destinies, we naturally long for a happiness and fulfillment we cannot orchestrate for ourselves. In contrast to the belief of some Christians throughout the centuries that real love forgets self entirely, the more common view of Christian love is far less stoic. It is in contrast a sturdy, earthy love that fully acknowledges the "not yet" pilgrim status of our existence. We are not perfected in this life; we continue to need in some measure until the moment of death. And out of this need arises sin, which never stops impeding our ability to love perfectly.

If we cannot forgive ourselves for this needy sinfulness and honestly declare, "It's good that you exist!" to the image in the mirror, how can we ever begin to forgive and love our equally weak brothers and sisters? For as Augustine reminds us, "If you do not know how to love yourself, you cannot truthfully love your neighbor."[16]

And thus, I saw, Isaiah's question—What does it mean to love your neighbor as yourself?—had been answered. That little towhead I'd repudiated and despised for so many decades had been the key to lots of things: my inability to forgive myself for being a flawed and often-unlikable human being, my inability to let go of a set of impossible standards, my inability to love and forgive others—even my inability to experience trustful joy. I'd taken a first step: I'd recognized her as the product of a childishly distorted imagination and consciously let her go. But could God teach me to love the other versions of myself? Rebellious teenager, restless twentysomething, ambitious thirty-year-old, overwhelmed stepmom in her forties? And could he teach me to love other people in the same way?

Then I thought of a possible exemplar, an Orthodox Jewish woman who converted to Catholicism in Germany during the years leading up to the Third Reich. Edith Stein, or St. Teresa Benedicta of the Cross, led an agape-infused life and suffered a martyr's death in the midst of horrific, unrestrained evil. To the moment of her death at age fifty-one in the concentration camp at Auschwitz, she steadily loved those God placed in her path, including her murderers. What's really amazing is that she had begun the way I did—as an intellectually arrogant young rebel—before embarking on her life-transforming way of the cross.

St. Teresa Benedicta of the Cross: Whom Love Transformed

Born in Breslau, Germany (now Wrocław, Poland), at the end of the nineteenth century on the Jewish Day of Atonement, Edith Stein, like Catherine of Siena and Thérèse of Lisieux, was the youngest of a large family. Her parents were devout Orthodox Jews; her great-grandfather had been a cantor and a prayer leader within their tightly bound community, and his wife a *mulier fortis*, or "woman of inner strength and authority."[17] As the eleventh child, Edith grew up surrounded by serious-minded adults and older siblings who religiously went to synagogue, made their daily prayers at home, and celebrated all Jewish holy days.

Her mother, Frau Auguste Stein, was a powerful influence on Edith during her growing-up years. Intelligent, strong, and determined, Auguste had already weathered the deaths of four children before her youngest was born, and shortly afterward, when the family lumber business began to fail, she had to leave her relatives and community in order to follow her husband to Breslau. There, at the age of forty-eight, he died suddenly of a stroke, leaving Auguste alone to support her remaining seven children. Edith was not yet two.

Auguste decided that the best way to make a living was to continue running the business on her own. Her long hours of work meant that her oldest daughter, Else, had to take on much of the child rearing. This was not such an easy task. "When things did not go her way," says one of her biographers, "her normal vivacity would express itself by means of temper tantrums. Even locking her in her room did no good at such moments: she simply continued annoying the rest of the family by banging her fists against the door."[18]

Edith also developed an "uncontrollable vanity," putting in her "two cents" when the grown-ups were trying to converse and generally showing off her intellect. Says a childhood friend, "When she didn't reach her goal—to prove she was the best and smartest—she vented her frustration in tears of rage. That wasn't so attractive."[19]

A mysterious change occurred when she was seven, however. The high-strung child became an overnight introvert, preferring to spend long hours alone thinking rather than trying to dominate the family conversations. It was as though she were now living in a separate world, isolated from the people she loved the most, particularly her mother. As she would later write, "In spite of the great closeness between us, I couldn't confide in my mother more than in anyone else. From early childhood I led a strange double life that produced alternations of behavior which must have seemed incomprehensible and erratic to any outside observer."[20]

Worse, her tendency toward temper tantrums now gave way to deep psychic distress. Fearful and hypersensitive, she seemed to have no inner defenses against outer sensory impressions. The sight of a poor person on the street would fill her with anguish, and an unkind word could set her trembling. Like her Carmelite predecessors Teresa of Ávila and Thérèse of Lisieux, she often ran mysterious high fevers. Yet "I never said a word about my secret sufferings to anyone. It just never occurred to me that you could talk about these things."[21]

Interestingly enough, Edith had little concern for God during these years. As her mother's daughter, she faithfully attended synagogue and participated in all required Jewish rituals, but her inner life remained unaffected by religion. The closest she could come to grasping what a relationship with God would be like was the love between her and her mother. Yet despite Edith's lack of spiritual motivation for change, she concluded when still young that she could no longer allow herself to be controlled by her emotions. She set out to learn self-discipline. Later, she would write by way of explanation that she feared losing "her spiritual freedom and personal dignity" by "letting herself go." The result was that "very early on [she] acquired so much self-control that [she] could remain constantly even-tempered without any great struggle."[22]

Yet she felt herself surrounded by adults who, despite how much they loved her, could not understand her and insisted upon treating her like a child. She felt strongly drawn to school, where she instantly flourished. She could not get enough of history and German in particular; she felt almost starved for knowledge and consumed books like food. Later she realized that this period had been crucial to her intellectual development. "Little by little, things started getting brighter and clearer in my inner world."[23]

At age thirteen, however, a new crisis hit. Psychologically depleted by her intense studies and emotionally exhausted by the realization that she had entirely lost her childhood faith and no longer believed in the existence of a personal God, she requested a leave from school. Her mother, concerned about her physical frailty, sent her to live with her now-married oldest sister, Else, who needed help with her small children. There Edith lived for eight months, quietly performing all the household and child-care tasks that were asked of her. At the end of this interlude, she was ready to return to her studies.

Now she concentrated on math and Latin, without any idea that this ancient language, which fascinated her and felt like her "native tongue," was the language of the church and someday she would be "praying in it." Still without God, she consciously adapted her mother's rigorous spiritual discipline to her own life. Auguste's quest for the divine was replaced by Edith's own quest for "the truth." She developed during this period the key qualities of her adult character: steadiness, reserve, kindness, self-discipline, thoughtfulness, and humility.[24]

As she approached graduation, it became clear that, given the family's financial circumstances, she needed to choose and pursue a career. Despite pressure from an uncle to become a doctor and go to work in the sanatorium he envisioned running, she remained firm in her resolve to follow her "inner drive" rather than succumb to other people's ideas for her life. She felt sure she was meant to teach, and she entered the University of Breslau in 1911. There she quickly became interested in the still relatively new field of psychology. During her seven years as an atheist, she had continued to ponder the problem of the soul as the center of the human person, and in psychology she saw the possibility of answering some of her questions.

She enrolled in courses taught by experimental psychologists and began writing papers from the viewpoint of cognitive psychology, but she soon became disappointed and even disillusioned. The focus in her chosen field was on human beings as bundles of sense impressions, not on human beings as unified spiritual entities, and the soul was no longer a necessary concept for researchers like Edith. In fact, "the entire notion of the soul had been relegated to the realm of the irrational and mythological, henceforth to be regarded with a skeptical smile."[25]

Then she came across the *Logical Investigations* of the phenomenologist Edmund Husserl, a brilliant Jewish thinker who was seeking to reconnect philosophy with its deepest root. Like Edith, Husserl had become skeptical about the scientific approach to philosophy because the area with which science concerns itself—the physical realm—does not include nonphysical things that clearly *are*: mental concepts, for example, or our own sense of self. Another problem for him was the lack of certainty inherent in all scientific claims. We can never prove something absolutely by using the scientific method—carefully observing things and then coming up with a probable explanation—for there always remains a chance that we have missed some bit of evidence that might invalidate the claim. Even worse, as Husserl saw it, was the effect of psychology on our beliefs about truth, and the notion that all knowledge ultimately arises from our "personal intuition of the world"[26] rather than from some reality outside our own minds.

Husserl concluded that the real subject of philosophy—the nature of being—could not be approached through the inexact methods of science or psychology at all. Instead, he directed his investigations toward discovering a way to the pure and "universally true" consciousness in which "Absolute Being" might manifest itself.[27] In the skeptical modern world, his focus on spirit made him an intriguing and controversial figure.

The spiritually starved Edith was riveted by Husserl's work and soon made plans to move to the University of Göttingen to study this new philosophy of phenomenology with him as her teacher. Surprisingly enough, Auguste gave her blessing, despite her sorrowful underlying intuition that her youngest daughter was leaving behind the world of traditional Judaism forever. As Edith began saying good-bye to her family, community, and university colleagues, most of whom were sad to see her go, she was taken aback by the unexpected parting comment of a good friend: "I hope in Göttingen you'll find people who measure up to your standards."[28]

As she puts it in her autobiography:

> I was living in the naive delusion common to so many people with no faith but with an exalted ethical idealism: that since I found goodness attractive, I personally must be good myself. I had always considered

it my right to take exception to anything that struck
me negatively, sometimes, even, in a mocking and
ironic way. There were actually people who considered me "delightfully malicious". So, to hear such
serious parting words from a man I respected and
loved came to me as a painful shock. . . . they were like
a trumpet call which forced me to start thinking.[29]

However, she soon became immersed in her new world of
Göttingen and philosophy. Husserl's exciting ideas had spurred
widespread intellectual discussion right at the moment when
"'Christian philosophy' was awaking like Sleeping Beauty from
its centuries-old sleep." By revitalizing the ancient tradition of the
"a priori knowledge of essences," he was setting himself against the
modern reigning philosophies of strict empiricism, skepticism, and
relativism, positions that by their nature are antithetical to Judeo-
Christian thought.[30]

Husserl believed that a passive intellect was a receptor for truth
from the objects that surrounded it—that the physical world,
in other words, could impart spiritual knowledge.[31] Many of his
readers saw here a connection with the medieval Scholasticism of
Aquinas, who believed that material objects were a combination of
formless matter and a variety of unchanging forms that had been
created by God.[32] In other words, what we touch, taste, see, hear,
and smell with our physical senses both exists in its own right and
is united with us through what we have in common: existence itself,
or being.[33] Husserl's students, without realizing it, were being prepared to take a serious new look at Christianity.

Edith herself found in Husserl's phenomenology a way to once
again focus on her primary question: what accounts for the unity
of the human person? This was both a metaphysical and an ethical
query for her. Not only was she still deeply interested in the nearly

outdated concept of soul, but she also wanted to find a way to live a good life. She suspected that a prerequisite for loving others was a unified self. As she wrote during this time, "Only the individual who experiences himself as a person, as an integrated whole, is capable of understanding other persons."[34] Yet she was fully aware of how the ego can delude us. Perhaps for this reason, she chose the nature of empathy as the subject of her dissertation: how can we know what it is like to be another?

Meanwhile, Husserl published a new book, this one with an obviously idealistic bent. The philosopher who had fought so long and hard on the side of realism, a position that had attracted to his circle some of the brightest young minds in Germany, now seemed to be abandoning his original thesis. His disciples, and particularly Edith, quickly realized that their master was moving on in a direction they could not follow. Shortly thereafter, she met Max Scheler, a brilliant young Jewish phenomenologist and convert to Christianity. She began attending his lectures on religious questions, one of which was entitled "The Nature of the Holy," and realized that here was a whole new world she'd never yet explored. Scheler taught that humility was the basis of morality and that the ultimate goal of the moral life was loss of self in God.[35]

As she would later write about her long training under Husserl, "All that constant drilling about looking at everything without prejudice and throwing away our blinders hadn't been in vain. The bars of the rationalist prejudices I had unconsciously grown up with [now] collapsed, and there, standing in front of me, was the world of faith."[36] It was Husserl's younger colleague Adolf Reinach who became Edith's exemplar at this point. She says about their first meeting, "Never before could I remember meeting anybody so absolutely good-hearted."[37] Later, she went to his home and became friends with his wife and sister, who not only reflected the same purity of heart but also humbled Edith intellectually with their intelligence and education. When World War I broke out, Reinach and his wife were baptized as Lutherans, and he wrote from his regiment that "in future his role as a philosopher would be to bring others to faith."[38]

As more and more of her friends were drafted into the army, Edith herself volunteered for duty at the Hospital for Infectious Diseases at Mährisch-Weisskirchen. Here she cared for very sick men suffering from a variety of ills: typhus, cholera, dysentery. When the war finally ended, she would be awarded the medal for valor, but more important to her at the time was what she had learned by the experience: that "dedication and not knowledge is of ultimate importance."[39]

In 1916, Husserl asked her to become his graduate assistant in Freiburg, where she finally completed the requirements for her doctorate. There she also received the news that Adolf Reinach had been killed on the fields of Flanders. Devastated, she went to Göttingen to help Reinach's young widow put his papers in order. To Edith's amazement, she found Frau Reinach calm, peaceful, and filled with a luminous hope. The last barrier to religion began crumbling within Edith. As she would later write to a Jesuit friend, "It was my first encounter with the Cross and the divine power that it bestows on those who carry it. For the first time, I was seeing with my very eyes the Church . . . triumphant over the sting of death."[40]

She called this an experience of the "mystery of the Cross" and felt her perspective dramatically shifting. She began reading the New Testament and immersing herself in a world where hope reigns over despair. Germany's string of military defeats ushered in an era of extreme pessimism; the suicide rate began to climb. Edith became quite concerned about several of her sisters, who seemed to be succumbing to the general spirit of depression. As she wrote in a letter to them, "Sometimes, I really believe that we have to get used to the idea that we may not survive the end of the war. But that's no excuse to despair either. If only we didn't limit our vision to the little bit of life in front of us, and then, only to what's immediately visible on the surface."[41]

Yet the intellectual struggle within her continued. She was still too invested in the search for truth to wholeheartedly embrace

She called this an experience of the "mystery of the Cross" and felt her perspective dramatically shifting.

the religious viewpoint. One night at the house of friends, however, she picked up a book: the *Life* of Teresa of Ávila. She could not put it down all night. The moment she finished reading, she knew that "this is the truth." According to her biographer, thanks to Teresa's *Life*, Edith had discovered that "God is not a God of knowledge, God is love. He does not reveal his mysteries to the deductive intelligence, but to the heart that surrenders itself to him."[42]

In 1922, Edith was baptized as a Catholic, and several months later she was confirmed. Secretly, she already knew that she was being called to become a Carmelite nun, like her mentor Teresa of Ávila, but she dared not tell her mother yet, who was still reeling with the shock of her daughter's conversion to Christianity. Instead, Edith went back to teaching, this time in a Dominican convent school in Speyer. About this far less prestigious post, she wrote, "The most important thing is that teachers really possess the Spirit of Christ and embody it in a living way."[43]

Along with giving herself to her young students, she became heavily involved with the poor of the city. Regarding Christian charity, she wrote, "On the question of relating to our fellow-men—our neighbor's spiritual need transcends every commandment. Everything else we do is a means to an end. But love is an end already, since God is love."[44]

Her most important activity during this time, however, was conducted mostly in secret: often she could not find a moment for prayer until late at night, when she would kneel in church for many hours. Later, she revealed what these silent vigils were about: "Prayer is the communication of the soul with God. God is love, and love is goodness giving itself away."[45] Her students later commented that her solitary nights of prayer, which she never spoke about in public but which became widely known within the convent community, provided one of the most powerful examples they'd ever had of what it meant to live in imitation of Christ.

Her contemplative practice led to her firm belief in the traditional Christian doctrine of deification. If we are not being transformed along the way, she was convinced, then all our preaching and service is in vain. She was careful to point out the difference between "leading the self-satisfied existence of the 'good Catholic' who 'does his duty', 'reads the right newspaper', and 'votes correctly'—and then does just as he pleases" and becoming a new man in Christ. The beginning of real transformation precipitates a difficult but lifesaving crisis: "If, up to now, a person has been more or less contented with himself, the time for that is over. He will do what he can to change the unpleasant things he finds in himself, but he will discover quite a bit that can't be called beautiful and yet will be nearly impossible to change. As a result he will slowly become small and humble, increasingly patient and tolerant toward the specks in his brothers' eyes."[46]

She was also careful to point out that her practice of solitary prayer was not an individualistic endeavor but entirely interlinked with the mission of the church. "The mystical current flowing down the centuries is not a divergent stream that has somehow been separated from the Church's life of prayer. On the contrary, it is its innermost life. Without it, there would be neither liturgy nor Church." Yet, conversely, "the mystic is simply the person who has an experiential knowledge of the teachings of the Church: that God dwells in the soul."[47]

In 1925, she was asked to make a translation of St. Thomas Aquinas's *Disputed Questions on Truth*, a work unfamiliar to phenomenologists. Immersing herself in Thomistic thought deepened her understanding of the Christian calling: "I have gradually come to the realization that something more is asked of us in this world, and that even in the contemplative life, one may not sever the link with the world. . . . The deeper one is drawn into God, the more he needs to go out of himself—out into the world, that is, to carry the divine life into it."[48]

Meanwhile, her intellectual reputation continued to grow. She began receiving invitations to lecture all over Germany and Europe, particularly on the subject of women in the modern world. Friends and colleagues, impressed with the international respect her work was beginning to command, urged her to apply for university professorships in Freiburg and Breslau. She was turned down in both places, despite her impeccable credentials, and it was only later that she understood what was going on: a more blatant and aggressive anti-Semitism was emerging in Germany.

While she was still waiting for responses to her applications, she was offered a lectureship at the German Institute for Scientific Pedagogy in Münster, which she ultimately accepted, despite the fact that she would once again be pulled away from her philosophical work. Within a year, however, the Nazis had come to power, and massive anti-Jewish persecutions began.[49] The fact that she was a Catholic working in a Catholic institution initially seemed to make her situation more favorable. But she herself intuited that a disaster of monstrous proportions was about to be unleashed upon her people, and she requested a private audience with the pope to warn him of the coming storm in Germany, hoping he would write a special encyclical that might help avert it. Her request for the audience was denied, so she wrote him a personal letter. He responded with blessings for her family. Her position at the institute was not renewed. Although she was disappointed, she wrote to a friend, "There's nothing to regret about the fact that I can't continue to lecture. To me a great and merciful Providence seems to be standing behind it all."[50] And in fact, it was the institutionalized anti-Semitism of the National Socialist Party that finally opened the door to monastic life, for God seemed to be slowly cutting off all other possible vocations. Two years later she publicly declared her intention of becoming a Carmelite nun. Her mother, now eighty-four, was inconsolable, and some of the saddest weeks of Edith's life were spent saying good-bye forever to her still-unreconciled mother. "It was a step that had to be taken in the absolute darkness of faith. Time and again, I asked myself during those weeks, 'Which of us is going to break first—me or my mother?' But the two of us held out to the very last day."[51]

The next morning she was on her way to the Carmel at Cologne, and immediately her spirits began to lift. She knew without a doubt that this was where God intended her to be for the rest of her life. As a novice of forty-two, she was considered old, and those at the convent privately wondered how she would adapt to the strict Carmelite regimen. Everything in her, however, responded joyfully to this new, intensely focused way of living, despite the sadness of her mother's death while Edith, now Sister Teresa Benedicta of the Cross, was still a junior professed nun.

Auguste's death was followed by the emigration of many Stein family members out of their increasingly hostile and dangerous homeland.[52] In 1938, the year Edith made her final vows at the Carmel of Cologne, the infamous Kristallnacht occurred—a systematic and deadly pogrom that served as a terrifying prophecy of what would become of the remaining Jews in Germany. Edith knew that as a Jewish convert to Catholicism she had a special role to fulfill in the coming days, and she wrote that she felt in some ways like the Old Testament Esther, meant to stand forth on behalf of her people.

Though Edith was already reconciled to her own fate, whatever it might be, her presence in the Carmel was putting the whole community in danger. The prioress made the difficult decision, with Edith in full agreement, to transfer her to the Carmel of Echt, in the Netherlands. In the middle of the night on the last day of the year, she was driven across the border to her new convent. She was deeply grateful for the sincere welcome she received there but wrote, "It's up to [God] how long I stay here and what will happen after that; these are things I don't need to worry about.[53]

In Echt, she became convinced that the magnitude of the disaster that lay before the world required deliberate acts of atonement, and on Passion Sunday 1939 she delivered this prayer to her mother superior: "Please permit me to offer myself to the Heart of Jesus as a sacrifice of atonement for true peace, that if possible the reign of Antichrist might be broken without another world war and a new social order might be established." The same year, she wrote her final testament: "I joyfully accept in advance the death God has appointed for me, in perfect submission to his most holy will."[54] She asked specifically that her death might serve to help the cause of the Jewish people.

Edith's sister Rosa managed to escape to Echt the following year, with the Germans not far behind her. The Netherlands was under full Nazi occupation by the close of 1940, and word began trickling in to the Carmel about the dissolution of monasteries in Germany. Edith could feel the end coming, yet when she was asked by the new prioress of the convent to write a book on St. John of the Cross, she obediently took up the project that would become *The Science of the Cross*. Immersing herself in the great Christian treatise on mystical death and resurrection, she awaited the arrival of her captors.

Regarding Jesus' injunction to "take up the cross and follow him," she wrote that "the Cross symbolize[s] all that is so oppressive and contrary to nature that it seems as hard as death. And the disciple of Jesus is to bear this burden daily."[55] In a chapter entitled "The Message of Scripture," she added, "Christ took upon himself the yoke of the Law by fulfilling it and by dying for and through the Law. Thus he freed from the Law those who want to receive life from him. But they can receive it only by surrendering their own life. For those who have been baptized in Christ have been baptized into his death."[56]

By now, the Dutch Jews were being interrogated by the SS, forced to wear the yellow star, and herded into trains bound for the east. The resistance from the Christian community in the Netherlands was strong, with many non-Jews voluntarily wearing the hated star themselves to demonstrate their solidarity with the Jewish cause. Church leaders in both the Catholic and Protestant communities joined forces and sent a telegram of protest to the German authorities. They, in return, promised to leave Jewish Christians alone if the churches would drop the issue. Instead, on July 26, 1942, the bishop of Utrecht authorized a pastoral letter that forcefully condemned the Nazi depredations. This was to be read aloud in all Catholic parishes.

Retaliation by the German authorities was swift. One week later, every Jewish Catholic in the Netherlands was arrested. Edith spent that day working on *The Science of the Cross*. Late in the afternoon, two SS officers appeared at the convent, demanding that she be ready to leave in five minutes. Stunned at the suddenness of this event she'd long expected, she packed and went to the convent gate, where Rosa was already waiting. Angry protesters were milling in the street outside, and Rosa began to look dazed. Edith, however, calmly reached for her hand, saying, "Come, Rosa. We're going for our people."[57]

From Echt, they were driven to a holding camp at Amersfoort, where fifteen members of other Catholic communities were being held along with more than a thousand Jews. The atmosphere was brutal and terrifying, and many of the women were deeply depressed. A survivor says, regarding Edith, "What I still recall very clearly is the unworried, or perhaps even cheerful, way that she and the other brothers and sisters accepted the situation. . . . They even took care of some of the children. This was so different from the attitude of the other prisoners, who seemed paralyzed with fear—and with good reason." [58]

Soon twelve hundred prisoners were loaded on the train to Westerbork, where even worse conditions prevailed. Here, spouses were deliberately separated, and "many of the mothers were on the brink of insanity." Children roamed the camp, hungry and dirty. Edith "immediately set about taking care of these little ones. She washed them, combed their hair, and tried to make sure they were fed and cared for." [59] Several days later, two men from Echt arrived at the camp with a packet of goods from the Carmel. They found Edith to be calm, quiet, and composed, imbued with a "lighthearted happiness" that was magnetic in the midst of such human misery. [60]

Another account of the hellhole of Westerbork says that the only word to describe Edith, "this middle-aged woman who struck everyone as so young, who was so whole and honest and genuine," was *saintly*. "When she spoke, it was impossible not to be moved by her humility and conviction. Talking with her was like . . . journeying into another world, where for the moment, Westerbork ceased to exist." [61]

In the predawn hours of August 7, thousands of inmates—almost the entire population of the camp—were awakened and directed to the train that would take them east to Auschwitz. Edith and Rosa were among them. Only a sketchy account remains of their last two days: a station official in Schifferstadt spoke briefly with Edith from the platform. She called to him from inside the tightly packed car and asked him to greet a local friend and pass on the news that she was "on her way to the east."[62]

There are no further records, except for a brief listing of her death at Auschwitz on August 9, along with everyone else on the transport from Westerbork. The effort to have her canonized began twenty years later, and in 1998, she was declared a saint.

In the book she was writing on the day she was arrested, she said:

> Many Christians feel depressed because the events of the Gospel do not—or do no longer—impress them as they ought and fail to affect and shape their lives. The example of the saints shows how it ought to be: where there is a truly living faith the Christian doctrine and the mighty deeds of God are the content of life which shape everything and before which everything else must give way. This is "holy objectivity", i.e., the original receptivity of a soul re-born by the Holy Spirit. Such a soul reacts to all events in the proper way and at the right depth; it has in itself a living, moving power joyfully ready to let itself be formed, unhampered by false inhibitions and rigidity. If a saintly soul thus assimilates the truths of the faith they become the science of the saints.[63]

Quietly, I laid down my books on Edith Stein, whose life and death had taught me all anyone needed to know about agape. The question was, how would this knowledge change me?

For several months, things went on as usual. Then, without knowing why, I felt a strong urge to reread my journals of the past thirty years, all stashed away in a couple of bottom drawers where I hoped no one else would ever find them. At first, I felt only embarrassment—what a stubborn, idealistic ignoramus I'd been! What a fool . . . and then, suddenly and unexpectedly, I felt an uprush of maternal tenderness, a desire to reach out and embrace this creature I'd once been, this baffling, exasperating young woman who'd kept growing and shedding skins faster than I could keep up with her. What had I been doing all these years, judging and condemning her for every misguided notion and mistake? Why had I thought it so important to sever our relationship, to disavow any connection with her?

I knew why. Only pride could cause such lovelessness. I'd been like the man Nietzsche described, so "addicted to honor" I couldn't accept love even from myself. Yet now I felt a joyful melting somewhere deep inside, as though I were reuniting with a beloved someone long since dead. And for a few moments I glimpsed the goodness of God's creation beneath its weight of sorrow and sin. Thanks, perhaps, to the intercession of Edith Stein, who despite her intellectualism firmly believed that only prayer and acts of atonement—not arguments—can change the human heart, maybe I'd finally been freed up to love.

Jesus' favorite disciple, John, may have summed up this uniquely Christian project best: "Dear friends, let us love one another, for love comes from God. Everyone who loves has been born of God and knows God. Whoever does not love does not know God, because God is love. . . . No one has ever seen God; but if we love one another, God lives in us and his love is made complete in us" (1 John 4:7–8, 12).

Remember always that you came here for no other
reason than to be a saint; thus, let nothing reign in
your soul that does not lead you to sanctity.
St. John of the Cross (1542–91)[1]

For years we had been putting up with a backyard bog. Somewhere in the hillside behind the house ran a hidden spring that soaked big portions of the lawn, even in the dry season, and made the grass difficult to mow. Worse, the standing water left us vulnerable to flooding during the big Pacific storms that sometimes rolled through. I had long been itching to dig into the hillside to find the source of the flow.

Then we did go through a small flood: one room soaked, a carpet ruined, and a computer nearly destroyed. Before rainy season began the following November, Mike marshaled "the guys" to help tackle the drainage problem. Joe rumbled up our driveway on the backhoe, and soon the boggy lawn was history. The rest of the guys showed up for their usual hearty breakfast, and by the end of the day, big ditches had been dug, pipes laid, and wheelbarrows of gravel dumped into the trenches. In the following weeks, Mike built a retaining wall, stone by stone, and a different Joe helped with a new irrigation system. Finally, we could stand back and admire our flood-proof backyard and the slender wands of baby grass that carpeted it.

But not for long. During the first big winter storm we could see that our admirable new French drains could not control the runoff from the hidden spring after all. Standing pools drowned the infant lawn. My just-planted rockroses, meant to droop romantically over the stone retaining wall, went into watery shock and died.

As soon as the rains stopped, and without consulting Mike first, I grimly went to work. I would find that spring, and no one could stop me. I dug into black, rotting soil, chipped away at sandstone, carted off unearthed rocks. I whanged away with the breaker bar until my wrists burned. Somewhere in that hillside lay the source of our liquid troubles.

Hunter, who rents a small apartment at the back of the house, was the first to discover me knee-deep in mud. She stood on her patio, hands on hips, watching me thoughtfully but without comment. Hunter is discreet. I called out, "I'm finding the spring."

"I thought so," she called back. "Need any help?"

"Thanks," I said, waving her off, "but this is a one-woman project."

Mike, who was thoroughly sick of the whole backyard after so many months of heavy work, didn't figure out what I was up to for a few more days. Then he squished across the lawn to take a look at the soggy hole in which I was working. "The spring?"

I nodded defensively. "I know it's in there somewhere. I've just got to get deeper."

He gave me a long look. "You know you can hurt your wrists with that breaker bar. Not to mention your back. Take it easy, okay?"

"I am," I lied. I was grateful he hadn't offered to help. For by now it was clearly a case of woman versus spring, and I didn't need any interference.

By the next afternoon, I had carved an eight-by-ten-foot gully into the side of the hill, and I knew I was getting warm. The water was streaming into the new sandstone pool so fast that I was standing shin-deep in it. Suddenly, I dug into a rock face with a long crack running through it, and I began poking my shovel along the fissure. Sure enough, here was a weak spot. I scratched away with my fingers till I'd made a hole; then, like a human gopher, I began to tunnel into the space behind the face.

Minutes later, with my arm buried halfway to the shoulder, I felt it: flowing water. I yelped with joy and looked around for an audience, but Hunter and Mike had long since lost interest in the project. My only witness was our cat Magpie, and she sprawled half-asleep under a redwood, clearly unimpressed.

I, however, was completely enchanted with my discovery. *The spring!* I kept thinking. *The spring!* Yet I knew it wasn't the flooding or the boggy lawn or the dead rockroses that had fueled this grandiose effort on my part. Nor were they responsible for my giddy excitement. Something else was at work here, although I wasn't quite sure what it was. I stood there puzzled in the mud. Then I remembered the words of that long-ago Byzantine monk. "It was like a spring," he said in regard to his already-praying, contemplative heart, "but one covered by a stone. Then at a certain moment Jesus took the stone away. At that the spring began to flow and has been flowing ever since."

The living waters, it seemed, were unstoppable, and I had proof here in my own backyard. God's work was going on in this world, and there was no curtailing it. All our human attempts to control or monitor the flow of divine love were doomed: there was nothing for it but to participate in the great transformative project going on beneath our noses.

Here, in this stubborn spring of ours, was a sign for me to remember: we are made for union with God, and the urge for that union is irresistible. When we live in a culture or era that denies the spiritual, as ours has done for so long, it is difficult to know what is happening to us when the Holy Spirit begins to shake the ground on which we stand. Yet this is the critical moment when we either accept our real identity and the grace that attends it or turn away in fearful self-protectiveness.

The apostle Paul is firm about this divine identity of ours: "So then you are no longer strangers and sojourners, but you are fellow citizens with the holy ones and members of the household of God, built upon the foundation of the apostles and prophets, with Christ Jesus himself as the capstone. Through him the whole structure is held together and grows into a temple sacred in the Lord; in him you also are being built together into a dwelling place of God in the Spirit" (Ephesians 2:19–22, NAB).

Before we can incorporate this knowledge into our way of being, however, we must learn to listen to our heart, that organ of prayer that is constantly communing with God, and we must develop the spiritual strength to handle an often-painful transformative process. Only then can God move us out of simple faithfulness and into the faith-filled holiness of the apostles and saints. Only then do we finally become what we were always meant to be.

For as St. Peter reminds us:

> [God's] divine power has bestowed on us everything that makes for life and devotion, through the knowledge of him who called us by his own glory and power. Through these, he has bestowed on us the precious and very great promises, so that through them you may come to share in the divine nature, after escaping form the corruption that is in the world because of evil desire. For this very reason, make every effort to supplement your faith with virtue, virtue with knowledge, knowledge with self-control, self-control with endurance, endurance with devotion, devotion with mutual affection, mutual affection with love. . . . For, in this way, entry into the eternal kingdom of our Lord and savior Jesus Christ will be richly provided for you. (2 Peter 1:3–7, 11, NAB)

NOTES

Introduction

1. Nikodimos of the Holy Mountain and Makarios of Corinth, *The Philokalia: The Complete Text*, trans. and ed. G. E. H. Palmer, Philip Sherrard, and Kallistos Ware (London: Faber and Faber, 1979), 1:206.

2. André Louf, *Teach Us to Pray*, trans. Hubert Hoskins (Cambridge, MA: Cowley Publications, 1992), 3.

Chapter 1: Prudence

1. Basil, *Exegetic Homilies*, trans. Agnes Clare Way, CDP, Fathers of the Church 46 (Washington, DC: Catholic University of America Press, 1963), 220.

2. Josef Pieper, *The Four Cardinal Virtues: Prudence, Justice, Fortitude, Temperance* (Notre Dame, IN: University of Notre Dame Press, 1966), 4.

3. Ibid., 6.

4. Georges Barrois, trans. and ed., *The Fathers Speak: St. Basil the Great, St. Gregory of Nazianzus, St. Gregory of Nyssa* (Crestwood, NY: St. Vladimir's Seminary Press, 1986), 26.

5. Ibid.

6. Basil, *Ascetical Works*, trans. M. Monica Wagner, CSC, The Fathers of the Church 9 (Washington, DC: Catholic University of America Press, 1962), vii.

7. Ibid.

8. Ibid., viii.

9. Barrois, *Fathers Speak*, 24.

10. Basil, *Ascetical Works*, 210.

11. Ibid., 248.

12. Ibid., 210.

13. Ibid., 12.

14. Ibid., ix–x.

15. Ibid., x–xi.

16. Ibid., 212.

17. Augustine Holmes, OSB, *A Life Pleasing to God: The Spirituality of the Rules of St. Basil* (London: Darton, Longman and Todd, 2000), 64.

18. Adalbert de Vogüé, OSB, "The Greater Rules of St. Basil—A Survey," in *In Honor of St. Basil the Great*, Word and Spirit 1 (Still River, MA: St. Bede's Publications, 1979), 52–53.

19. Vladimir Lossky, *The Mystical Theology of the Eastern Church*, trans. members of the Fellowship of St. Alban and St. Sergius (Crestwood, NY: St. Vladimir's Seminary Press, 2002), 124.

20. *Catechism of the Catholic Church* (Liguori: Liguori Publications, 1994), 116, no. 460.

21. Barrois, *Fathers Speak*, 47–8.

22. Ibid., 48.

23. Cyril Karam, OSB, "St. Basil on the Holy Spirit—Some Aspects of His Theology," in *In Honor of St. Basil the Great*, Word and Spirit 1 (Still River, MA: St. Bede's Publications, 1979), 159.

24. Ibid., 162.

25. Ibid., 159.

26. Ibid., 162–63.

27. *Catechism*, 116, no. 460.

28. John of the Cross, *The Collected Works of Saint John of the Cross*, trans. Kieran Kavanaugh, OCD, and Otilio Rodriguez, OCD, rev. ed. (Washington, DC: Institute of Carmelite Studies, 1991), 93.

29. Simon Chan, *Spiritual Theology: A Systematic Study of the Christian Life* (Downers Grove, IL: InterVarsity Press, 1998), 99.

30. Charles Taylor, *Sources of the Self: The Making of the Modern Identity* (Cambridge, MA: Harvard University Press, 1989), 16.

31. Pieper, *Four Cardinal Virtues*, 23.

32. Ibid., 22.

33. Ibid., 30.

34. Martha Nussbaum, *Upheavals of Thought: The Intelligence of Emotions* (Cambridge: Cambridge University Press, 2001).

35. Basil, *Exegetic Homilies*, 222.

Chapter 2: Temperance

1. R. A. Markus, *Gregory the Great and His World* (Cambridge: Cambridge University Press, 1997), 24.

2. Plato, *Symposium*, in *The Dialogues of Plato*, trans. Seth Bernadette (New York: Bantam, 1986), 265.

3. Ibid., 269.

4. Iris Murdoch, *Existentialists and Mystics: Writings on Philosophy and Literature* (New York: Allen Lane, 1998), 416.

5. Ibid., 417.

6. Ronald Rolheiser, *The Holy Longing: The Search for a Christian Spirituality* (New York: Doubleday, 1999), 4.

7. Ibid., 7.

8. Ibid., 22.

9. Brian Wilkie and James Hurt, comps., *Literature of the Western World*, vol. 2, *Neoclassicism through the Modern Period*, 4th ed. (Upper Saddle River, NJ: Prentice Hall, 1992), 668–799.

10. Josef Pieper, *The Four Cardinal Virtues: Prudence, Justice, Fortitude, Temperance* (Notre Dame, IN: University of Notre Dame Press, 1966), 146.

11. Ibid., 147–48.

12. Rolheiser, *Holy Longing*, 29.

13. Pieper, *Four Cardinal Virtues*, 148.

14. Ibid., 147.

15. Bernard McGinn, *The Doctors of the Church: Thirty-Three Men and Women Who Shaped Christianity* (New York: Crossroad, 1999), 86.

16. Ibid., 84.

17. Carole Straw, *Gregory the Great: Perfection in Imperfection* (Berkeley: University of California Press, 1988), 2.

18. Ibid.

19. Ibid., 3.

20. Ibid., 5.

21. McGinn, *Doctors of the Church*, 84.

22. Markus, *Gregory the Great*, 25.

23. Ibid., 24–25.

24. Ibid., 32.

25. Straw, *Gregory the Great*, 5.

26. Ibid., 41.

27. Gregory the Great, *Forty Gospel Homilies*, trans. Dom David Hurst, Cistercian Studies 123 (Kalamazoo, MI: Cistercian Publications, 1990), 89.

28. Straw, *Gregory the Great*, 93.

29. Ibid., 48.

30. Ibid., 92.

Chapter 3: Fortitude

1. Bernard of Clairvaux, *Bernard of Clairvaux: Selected Works*, trans. G. R. Evans (New York: Paulist Press, 1987), 85.

2. Josef Pieper, *The Four Cardinal Virtues: Prudence, Justice, Fortitude, Temperance* (Notre Dame, IN: University of Notre Dame Press, 1966), 121.

3. William James, *The Varieties of Religious Experience: A Study in Human Nature* (New York: Collier Books, 1961), 140.

4. Ibid., 135.

5. Evelyn Underhill, *Mysticism: The Nature and Development of Spiritual Consciousness* (Oxford: Oneworld Publications, 1993), 400.

6. Morton Kelsey, *Companions on the Inner Way: The Art of Spiritual Guidance*, 2nd ed. (New York: Crossroad, 1996), 150.

7. Ibid.

8. Pieper, *Four Cardinal Virtues*, 117.

9. Ibid.

10. Ibid.

11. Ibid., 117–18.

12. Ibid., 119.

13. Ibid., 123.

14. Ibid., 122.

15. Ibid., 129.

16. Ibid., 128.

17. Ibid., 136.

18. Ibid., 137.

19. Adriaan Bredero, *Bernard of Clairvaux: Between Cult and History* (Grand Rapids, MI: William B. Eerdmans, 1996), 203. Evans and Bredero do not agree on the birth date of Bernard, and I have chosen to go with Bredero.

20. Bernard of Clairvaux, *Selected Works*, 14 Richard Tarnas, *The Passion of the Western Mind: Understanding the Ideas That Have Shaped Our World View* (New York: Ballantine Books, 1991), 177.

21. Bernard of Clairvaux, *Selected Works*, 15–16.

22. Aelred Squire, OP, *Aelred of Rievaulx: A Study* (London: S.P.C.K., 1981), 17.

23. Bredero, *Bernard of Clairvaux*, 203. Evans and Bredero do not agree on this date, and I have chosen to go with Bredero.

24. Ibid., 212.

25. Squire, *Aelred of Rievaulx*, 17.

26. Bernard of Clairvaux, *Selected Works*, 17.

27. Ibid., 101.

28. Ibid., 101–2.

29. Ibid., 125–26.

30. Andrew Delbanco, *The Death of Satan: How Americans Have Lost the Sense of Evil* (New York: Farrar, Straus and Giroux, 1995), 23.

31. Ibid., 28.

32. Bredero, *Bernard of Clairvaux*, 195.

33. Bernard of Clairvaux, *Selected Works*, 284.

34. Bredero, *Bernard of Clairvaux*, 188.

35. Bernard of Clairvaux, *Selected Works*, 47.

36. Ibid., 46.

37. Ibid., 50.

38. Ibid., 42.

39. Ibid., 54.

40. Ibid., 36.

41. Peter Kreeft, *Christianity for Modern Pagans: Pascal's Pensées Edited, Outlined, and Explained* (San Francisco: Ignatius Press, 1966), 145.

42. Ibid., 79.

43. Rudolf Otto, *The Idea of the Holy*, trans. John W. Harvey (London: Oxford University Press, 1971), 10.

44. Bernard of Clairvaux, *Selected Works*, 37.

45. Ibid.

46. Mary Margaret Funk, OSB, *Thoughts Matter: The Practice of the Spiritual Life* (New York: Continuum, 1999), 9.

47. Otto, *Idea of the Holy*, 28.

48. Bernard of Clairvaux, *Selected Works*, 226.

49. Kelsey, *Companions*, 113.

Chapter 4: Justice

1. Albert the Great and Thomas Aquinas, *Albert and Thomas: Selected Writings*, trans. and ed. Simon Tugwell, OP (New York: Paulist Press, 1988), 543.

2. Josef Pieper, *The Four Cardinal Virtues: Prudence, Justice, Fortitude, Temperance* (Notre Dame, IN: University of Notre Dame Press, 1966), 43–44.

3. Ibid., 50.

4. Thomas Aquinas, *Summa Theologiae: A Concise Translation*, ed. Timothy McDermott (London: Methuen, 1989), 385.

5. Pieper, *Four Cardinal Virtues*, 8.

6. Aquinas, *Summa Theologiae*, 386.

7. Ibid., 394.

8. Ibid., 386.

9. Ibid., 387. Shaken by the knowledge that I had unjustly judged two good people, I turned for guidance to the saint who had shed so much light on this weakness of mine. I began to read about the life of St. Thomas Aquinas, who wrote extensively about the virtues.

10. James A. Weisheipl, OP, *Friar Thomas D'Aquino: His Life, Thought, and Work* (Garden City, NY: Doubleday, 1974), 9.

11. Ibid., 10.

12. Ibid., 13.

13. Ibid., 16.

14. Albert the Great and Aquinas, *Albert and Thomas*, 258.

15. W. T. Jones, *A History of Western Philosophy*, vol. 2, *The Medieval Mind*, 2nd ed. (New York: Harcourt, Brace and World, 1969), 68–69.

16. Weisheipl, *Friar Thomas D'Aquino*, 22–23.

17. Ibid., 22.

18. Thomas Aquinas, *An Aquinas Reader*, ed. Mary T. Clark (Garden City, NY: Image Books, 1972), 12.

19. Weisheipl, *Friar Thomas D'Aquino*, 27.

20. Ibid., 30.

21. Bernard McGinn, *The Doctors of the Church: Thirty-Three Men and Women Who Shaped Christianity* (New York: Crossroad, 1999), 117.

22. Ibid., 127.

23. Ibid., 125.

24. Aquinas, *An Aquinas Reader*, 9.

25. McGinn, *Doctors of the Church*, 127.

26. G. K. Chesterton, *Saint Thomas Aquinas: "The Dumb Ox"* (Garden City, NY: Image, 1956), 20.

27. Jones, *The Medieval Mind*, 209.

28. Aquinas, *An Aquinas Reader*, 12.

29. Ibid., 13.

30. Ibid., 14.

31. Chesterton, *Saint Thomas Aquinas*, 126.

32. Ibid., 126–27.

33. *Catechism of the Catholic Church* (Liguori: Liguori Publications, 1994), 44, no. 160.

34. Pieper, *Four Cardinal Virtues*, 113.

35. Albert the Great and Aquinas, *Albert and Thomas*, 264.

36. Chesterton, *Saint Thomas Aquinas*, 142.

Chapter 5: Humility

1. Teresa of Ávila, *The Collected Works of St. Teresa of Ávila*, vol 1, *The Book of Her Life, Spiritual Testimonies, Soliloquies*, trans. Kieran Kavanaugh, OCD and Otilio Rodriguez, OCD (Washington, DC: Institute of Carmelite Studies, 1976), 96–97.

2. David Daniels and Virginia Price, *The Essential Enneagram: The Definitive Personality Test and Self-Discovery Guide* (San Francisco: HarperSanFrancisco, 2000), 1.

3. Mary Margaret Funk, OSB, *Thoughts Matter: The Practice of the Spiritual Life* (New York: Continuum, 1999), 111.

4. Ibid., 113.

5. Josef Pieper, *The Four Cardinal Virtues: Prudence, Justice, Fortitude, Temperance* (Notre Dame, IN: University of Notre Dame Press, 1966), 189.

6. Funk, *Thoughts Matter*, 112.

7. Albert the Great and Thomas Aquinas, *Albert and Thomas: Selected Writings*, trans. and ed. Simon Tugwell, OP (New York: Paulist Press, 1988), 546.

8. Pieper, *Four Cardinal Virtues*, 189.

9. Adalbert de Vogüé, OSB, *The Rule of Saint Benedict: A Doctrinal and Spiritual Commentary*, trans. John Baptist Hasbrouck, Cistercian Studies 54 (Kalamazoo, MI: Cistercian Publications, 1983), 119–20.

10. Pieper, *Four Cardinal Virtues*, 190.

11. Paul Delatte, OSB, *The Holy Rule of St. Benedict: A Commentary*, trans. Dom Justin McCann (Latrobe, PA: Archabbey Press, 1959), 100–127.

12. Teresa of Ávila, *Collected Works*, 1.

13. Cathleen Medwick, *Teresa of Ávila: The Progress of a Soul* (New York: Image, 1999), 12.

14. Teresa of Ávila, *Collected Works*, 1.

15. Ibid., 6.

16. Ibid., 34.

17. Ibid., 35.

18. Ibid., 36.

19. Ibid., 38–39.

20. Ibid., 39–40.

21. Ibid., 41.
22. Ibid.
23. Medwick, *Teresa of Ávila*, 26.
24. Teresa of Ávila, *Collected Works*, 48.
25. Medwick, *Teresa of Ávila*, 31.
26. Teresa of Ávila, *Collected Works*, 54.
27. Ibid., 56.
28. Ibid., 64.
29. Ibid., 84.
30. Ibid., 86–87.
31. Teresa of Ávila, *The Interior Castle*, trans. and ed. E. Allison Peers (Garden City, NY: Image Books, 1961), 66.
32. Teresa of Ávila, *Collected Works*, 84.
33. Ibid., 87.
34. Ibid., 84–85.
35. Ibid., 85.
36. Ibid., 90.
37. Ibid., 93–94.
38. Teresa of Ávila, *The Interior Castle*, 66.
39. Teresa of Ávila, *Collected Works*, 359.
40. Ibid.
41. Ibid., 113.
42. Ibid., 105.

Chapter 6: Faith

1. Francis de Sales, *Introduction to the Devout Life*, trans. and ed. John K. Ryan, 2nd ed. (New York: Image, 1966), 283.
2. Josef Pieper, *Faith, Hope, Love* (San Francisco: Ignatius Press, 1997), 23.
3. Ibid., 22.
4. Pieper, *Faith, Hope, Love*, 24.
5. Ibid., 37.
6. Ibid., 40.
7. Pieper, *Faith, Hope, Love*, 40.
8. Ibid., 42.
9. Ibid., 64.

10. C. S. Lewis, *Miracles: A Preliminary Study* (San Francisco: HarperSanFrancisco, 1996), 150.

11. Robert Coles, *The Secular Mind* (Princeton, NJ: Princeton University Press, 1999), 30.

12. Ibid., 24.

13. *The Catholic Encyclopedia Online*, s.v. "St. Francis de Sales," http://www.newadvent.org/cathen/index.html.

14. Bernard McGinn, *The Doctors of the Church: Thirty-Three Men and Women Who Shaped Christianity* (New York: Crossroad, 1999), 160.

15. J. Leslie Dunstan, *Protestantism* (New York: George Braziller, 1961), 76.

16. McGinn, *Doctors of the Church*, 160.

17. Ibid.

18. Ibid., 161.

19. *The Catholic Encyclopedia Online*, s.v. "St. Francis de Sales."

20. McGinn, *Doctors of the Church*, 161.

21. Dunstan, *Protestantism*, 26.

22. *The Catholic Encyclopedia Online*, s.v. "St. Francis de Sales."

23. Francis de Sales, *The Catholic Controversy: St. Francis de Sales' Defense of the Faith*, trans. Henry Benedict Mackey, OSB (Rockford, IL: Tan Books and Publishers, 1989), xli.

24. Ibid.

25. Ibid., li.

26. Ibid., xlix.

27. Ibid., 11.

28. Ibid., 6.

29. Ibid., 7.

30. Ibid., 3.

31. Ibid., xlix.

32. Ibid., xlvi.

33. Ibid., liii.

34. Ibid., xlvii.

35. McGinn, *Doctors of the Church*, 161.

36. Francis de Sales, *Treatise on the Love of God*, trans. Henry Benedict Mackey, OSB (Rockford, IL: Tan Books and Publishers, 1997), 23–24.

37. Ibid., 25.

38. Ibid., 29.

39. Ibid., 30.

40. Ibid., 102.
41. Ibid., 103.
42. Ibid., 30.
43. Ibid., 32.
44. Pieper, *Faith, Hope, Love*, 37.
45. De Sales, *Love of God*, 104.
46. Pieper, *Faith, Hope, Love*, 39.
47. De Sales, *Love of God*, 243–44.
48. Ibid., 244–45.
49. Ibid., 245.
50. Ibid., 255.
51. Ibid., 259.
52. Ibid.
53. De Sales, *Devout Life*, 33.
54. Ibid., 34.

Chapter 7: Hope

1. Guy Gaucher, *The Passion of Thérèse of Lisieux* (New York: Crossroad, 2001), 56.
2. Josef Pieper, *Faith, Hope, Love* (San Francisco: Ignatius Press, 1997), 91.
3. Amédée Hallier, OCSO, *The Monastic Theology of Aelred of Rievaulx: An Experiential Theology*, trans. Columban Heaney, OCSO (Shannon: Irish University Press, 1969), 13.
4. Ibid., 36.
5. Ronald Rolheiser, *The Holy Longing: The Search for a Christian Spirituality* (New York: Doubleday, 1999), 1.
6. Ibid., 3.
7. G. K. Chesterton, *Orthodoxy* (San Francisco: Ignatius Press, 1995), 86.
8. Pieper, *Faith, Hope, Love*, 95.
9. Ibid., 97.
10. Ibid., 101.
11. Ibid., 99.
12. Ibid., 106.
13. Ibid., 107.
14. Ibid., 110–11.
15. Ibid., 114–15.

16. Mary Margaret Funk, OSB, *Thoughts Matter: The Practice of the Spiritual Life* (New York: Continuum, 1999), 93–94.

17. Susan Helen Wallace, FSP, *Saint Thérèse of Lisieux: With Confidence and Love* (Boston: Pauline Books and Media, 1998), 13–14.

18. Ibid., 17.

19. Thérèse of Lisieux, *Story of a Soul: The Autobiography of St. Thérèse of Lisieux*, trans. John Clarke, OCD, 3rd ed. (Washington, DC: Institute of Carmelite Studies, 1996), 6.

20. Ibid., 17.

21. Ibid., 28–29.

22. Ibid., 33.

23. Ibid., 36.

24. Ibid.

25. Ibid., 37.

26. Ibid., 59.

27. Ibid., 61–62.

28. Ibid., 65–66.

29. Ibid., 97.

30. Ibid., 98.

31. Ibid.

32. Ibid., 99.

33. Ibid., 100.

34. Ibid., 134–35.

35. Ibid., 148–49.

36. Ibid., 149.

37. Ibid., 150.

38. Ibid., 166.

39. Ibid., 171.

40. Ibid., 207.

41. Ibid., 208.

42. Ibid., 210.

43. Ibid., 218.

44. Gaucher, *Passion of Thérèse*, 39.

45. Thérèse of Lisieux, *Story of a Soul*, 213.

46. Gaucher, *Passion of Thérèse*, 57.

47. Ibid., 82.

48. Ibid., 87–88.

49. Ibid., 92–93.

50. Ibid., 120.

51. Ibid., 93.

52. Ibid., 94–95.

53. Pieper, *Faith, Hope, Love*, 136–37.

Chapter 8: Charity

1. Edith Stein, *Edith Stein: Essential Writings*, selected by John Sullivan, OCD, Modern Spiritual Masters (New York: Orbis Books, 2002), 42.

2. Aelred Squire, OP, *Aelred of Rievaulx: A Study* (London: S.P.C.K., 1981), 9.

3. Josef Pieper, *Faith, Hope, Love* (San Francisco: Ignatius Press, 1997), 163–64.

4. Ibid., 164–65.

5. Ibid., 174.

6. Ibid., 176

7. Ibid., 179.

8. Ibid., 180.

9. Ibid., 183.

10. Ibid., 186.

11. Ibid., 217.

12. Ibid., 218.

13. Ibid., 224.

14. Ibid., 226.

15. Ibid., 228.

16. Ibid., 237.

17. Waltraud Herbstrith, OCD, *Edith Stein: A Biography*, trans. Bernard Bonowitz, OCSO (San Francisco: Ignatius Press, 1992), 19.

18. Ibid., 21.

19. Ibid.

20. Ibid., 22.

21. Ibid.

22. Ibid., 23–24.

23. Ibid., 25.

24. Ibid., 27–28.

25. Ibid., 33.

26. Paul Strathern, *Heidegger in 90 Minutes* (Chicago: Ivan R. Dee, 2002), 21.

27. Ibid., 24.

28. Herbstrith, *Edith Stein*, 36.

29. Ibid.

30. Ibid., 39.

31. Ibid., 40.

32. C. E. M. Joad, *Guide to Philosophy* (New York: Dover Publications, 1936), 308.

33. Étienne Gilson, *Thomist Realism and the Critique of Knowledge*, trans. Mark A. Wauck (San Francisco: Ignatius Press, 1983), 10.

34. Herbstrith, *Edith Stein*, 42.

35. Ibid., 47.

36. Ibid., 48.

37. Ibid., 49.

38. Ibid., 51.

39. Ibid., 53.

40. Ibid., 56.

41. Ibid., 58.

42. Ibid., 64–65.

43. Ibid., 76.

44. Ibid., 79.

45. Stein, *Essential Writings*, 119.

46. Herbstrith, *Edith Stein*, 154.

47. Ibid., 157.

48. Ibid., 82.

49. Edith Stein, *The Science of the Cross: A Study of St. John of the Cross*, ed. L. Gelber and Romaeus Leuven, OCD, trans. Hilda Graef (Chicago: Henry Regnery Company, 1960), xiii.

50. Herbstrith, *Edith Stein*, 119–20.

51. Ibid., 122.

52. Stein, *Essential Writings*, 19.

53. Herbstrith, *Edith Stein*, 167.

54. Ibid., 168.

55. Stein, *Science of the Cross*, 7.

56. Ibid., 10.

57. Herbstrith, *Edith Stein*, 180.

58. Ibid., 181.
59. Ibid., 183.
60. Ibid., 185.
61. Ibid., 186.
62. Ibid., 189.
63. Stein, *Science of the Cross*, 2.

Epilogue

1. John of the Cross, *The Collected Works of Saint John of the Cross*, trans. Kieran Kavanaugh, OCD, and Otilio Rodriguez, OCD, rev. ed. (Washington, DC: Institute of Carmelite Studies, 1991), 729.

BIBLIOGRAPHY

Albert the Great and Thomas Aquinas. *Albert and Thomas: Selected Writings.* Translated and edited by Simon Tugwell, OP. New York: Paulist Press, 1988.

Aquinas, Thomas. *An Aquinas Reader.* Edited by Mary T. Clark. Garden City, NY: Image Books, 1972.

———. *Summa Theologiae: A Concise Translation.* Edited by Timothy McDermott. London: Methuen, 1989.

Aristotle. *The Philosophy of Aristotle.* Edited by Renford Bambrough. Translated by A. E. Wardman and J. L. Creed. New York: Mentor Books, 1963.

Barrois, Georges, trans. and ed. *The Fathers Speak: St. Basil the Great, St. Gregory of Nazianzus, St. Gregory of Nyssa.* Crestwood, NY: St. Vladimir's Seminary Press, 1986.

Basil. *Ascetical Works.* Translated by M. Monica Wagner, CSC. The Fathers of the Church 9. Washington, DC: Catholic University of America Press, 1962.

———. *Exegetic Homilies.* Translated by Agnes Clare Way, CDP. The Fathers of the Church 46. Washington, DC: Catholic University of America Press, 1963.

———. *Letters.* Vol. 1. Translated by Agnes Clare Way, CDP. The Fathers of the Church 13. New York: Fathers of the Church, 1951.

Bernard of Clairvaux. *Bernard of Clairvaux: Selected Works.* Translated by G. R. Evans. New York: Paulist Press, 1987.

St. Bernard of Clairvaux. Word and Spirit 12. Petersham, MA: St. Bede's Publications, 1990.

Bredero, Adriaan. *Bernard of Clairvaux: Between Cult and History.* Grand Rapids, MI: William B. Eerdmans, 1996.

Carluccio, Gerard G., OSB. *The Seven Steps to Spiritual Perfection: According to St. Gregory the Great.* Ottawa: University of Ottawa Press, 1949.

Catechism of the Catholic Church. Liguori, MO: Liguori Publications, 1994.

Chan, Simon. *Spiritual Theology: A Systematic Study of the Christian Life.* Downers Grove, IL: InterVarsity Press, 1998.

Chesterton, G. K. *Orthodoxy.* San Francisco: Ignatius Press, 1995.

————. *Saint Thomas Aquinas: "The Dumb Ox."* Garden City, NY: Image Books, 1956.

Coles, Robert. *The Secular Mind.* Princeton, NJ: Princeton University Press, 1999.

Copleston, F. C. *Aquinas.* Harmondsworth, Middlesex: Penguin Books, 1955.

Daniels, David, and Virginia Price. *The Essential Enneagram: The Definitive Personality Test and Self-Discovery Guide.* San Francisco: HarperSanFrancisco, 2000.

Delatte, Paul, OSB. *The Holy Rule of St. Benedict: A Commentary.* Translated by Dom Justin McCann. Latrobe, PA: Archabbey Press, 1959.

Delbanco, Andrew. *The Death of Satan: How Americans Have Lost the Sense of Evil.* New York: Farrar, Straus and Giroux, 1995.

De Sales, Francis. *The Catholic Controversy: St. Francis de Sales' Defense of the Faith.* Translated by Henry Benedict Mackey, OSB. Rockford, IL: Tan Books and Publishers, 1989.

————. *Introduction to the Devout Life.* Translated and edited by John K. Ryan. 2nd ed. New York: Image, 1972.

————. *Treatise on the Love of God.* Translated by Henry Benedict Mackey, OSB. Rockford, IL: Tan Books and Publishers, 1997.

Dunstan, J. Leslie. *Protestantism.* New York: George Braziller, 1961.

Egan, Harvey D., SJ. *Karl Rahner: The Mystic of Everyday Life.* New York: Crossroad, 1998.

Funk, Mary Margaret, OSB. *Thoughts Matter: The Practice of the Spiritual Life.* New York: Continuum, 1999.

Gaucher, Guy. *The Passion of Thérèse of Lisieux.* New York: Crossroad, 2001.

Gilson, Étienne. *The Mystical Theology of Saint Bernard.* Translated by A. H. C. Downes. New York: Sheed and Ward, 1940.

———. *The Spirit of Medieval Philosophy.* Translated by A. H. C. Downes. Notre Dame, IN: University of Notre Dame Press, 1991.

———. *Thomist Realism and the Critique of Knowledge.* Translated by Mark A. Wauck. San Francisco: Ignatius Press, 1986

Gratton, Carolyn. *The Art of Spiritual Guidance: A Contemporary Approach to Growing in the Spirit.* New York: Crossroad, 1993.

Gregory the Great. *Dialogues.* Translated by Odo John Zimmerman, OSB. The Fathers of the Church 39. New York: Fathers of the Church, 1959.

———. *Forty Gospel Homilies.* Translated by Dom David Hurst. Cistercian Studies 123. Kalamazoo, MI: Cistercian Publications, 1990.

———. *Morals on the Book of Job.* Vols. 2 and 3. Oxford: John Henry Parker, 1845.

———. *Pastoral Care.* Translated by Henry Davis, SJ. Ancient Christian Writers: The Works of the Fathers in Translation 11 Westminster, MD: Newman Press, 1955.

Hallier, Amédée, OCSO. *The Monastic Theology of Aelred of Rievaulx: An Experiential Theology.* Translated by Columban Heaney, OCSO. Translations from Aelred's works by Hugh McCaffery, OCSO. Shannon: Irish University Press, 1969.

Herbstrith, Waltraud, OCD. *Edith Stein: A Biography.* Translated by Bernard Bonowitz, OCSO. San Francisco: Ignatius Press, 1992.

Holmes, Augustine, OSB. *A Life Pleasing to God: The Spirituality of the Rules of St. Basil.* London: Darton, Longman and Todd, 2000.

Huxley, Aldous. *The Perennial Philosophy.* New York: Harper and Row, 1944.

James, William. *The Varieties of Religious Experience: A Study in Human Nature.* New York: Collier Books, 1961.

Joad, C. E. M. *Guide to Philosophy.* New York: Dover Publications, 1936.

John of the Cross. *The Collected Works of Saint John of the Cross.* Translated by Kieran Kavanaugh, OCD, and Otilio Rodriguez, OCD. Rev. ed. Washington, DC: Institute of Carmelite Studies, 1991.

Jones, W. T. *The Medieval Mind.* Vol. 2 of *A History of Western Philosophy.* 2nd ed. New York: Harcourt, Brace and World, 1969.

Karam, Cyril, OSB. "St. Basil on the Holy Spirit—Some Aspects of His Theology." In *In Honor of St. Basil the Great.* Word and Spirit 1. Still River, MA: St. Bede's Publications, 1979.

Kelsey, Morton. *Companions on the Inner Way: The Art of Spiritual Guidance.* 2nd ed. New York: Crossroad, 1996.

Kreeft, Peter. *Christianity for Modern Pagans: Pascal's Pensées Edited, Outlined, and Explained.* Selections from Pascal's *Pensées* translated by A. J. Krailsheimer. San Francisco: Ignatius Press, 1966.

Lewis, C. S. *Miracles: A Preliminary Study.* San Francisco: HarperSanFrancisco, 1996.

———. *The Screwtape Letters.* Uhrichville, OH: Barbour and Company, 1990.

Lossky, Vladimir. *The Mystical Theology of the Eastern Church.* Translated from the French by members of the Fellowship of St. Alban and St. Sergius. Crestwood, NY: St. Vladimir's Seminary Press, 2002.

Louf, André. *Teach Us to Pray*. Translated by Hubert Hoskins. Cambridge, MA: Cowley Publications, 1992.

Manss, Virginia, and Mary Frohlich, eds. *The Lay Contemplative: Testimonies, Perspectives, Resources*. Cincinnati: St. Anthony Messenger Press, 2000.

Markus, R. A. *Gregory the Great and His World*. Cambridge: Cambridge University Press, 1997.

McGinn, Bernard. *The Doctors of the Church: Thirty-Three Men and Women Who Shaped Christianity*. New York: Crossroad, 1999.

Medwick, Cathleen. *Teresa of Ávila: The Progress of a Soul*. New York: Image, 1999.

Murdoch, Iris. *Existentialists and Mystics: Writings on Philosophy and Literature*. New York: Allen Lane, 1998.

Nikodimos of the Holy Mountain and Makarios of Corinth. *The Philokalia: The Complete Text*. Vol. 1. Translated and edited by G. E. H. Palmer, Philip Sherrard, and Kallistos Ware. London: Faber and Faber, 1979.

———. *Writings from the Philokalia on Prayer of the Heart*. Translated by E. Kadloubovsky and G. E. H. Palmer. London: Faber and Faber, 1951.

Otto, Rudolf. *The Idea of the Holy*. Translated by John W. Harvey. London: Oxford University Press, 1971.

Pieper, Josef. *Faith, Hope, Love*. San Francisco: Ignatius Press, 1997.

———. *The Four Cardinal Virtues: Prudence, Justice, Fortitude, Temperance*. Notre Dame, IN: University of Notre Dame Press, 1966.

Plato. *Symposium*. In *The Dialogues of Plato*. Translated by Seth Bernadette. New York: Bantam, 1986.

Rolheiser, Ronald. *The Holy Longing: The Search for a Christian Spirituality*. New York: Doubleday, 1999.

Squire, Aelred, OP. *Aelred of Rievaulx: A Study*. Kalamazoo, MI: Cistercian Publications, 1981.

Stein, Edith. *Edith Stein: Essential Writings*. Selected by John Sullivan, OCD. Modern Spiritual Masters. New York: Orbis Books, 2002.

———. *The Science of the Cross: A Study of St. John of the Cross*. Edited by L. Gelber and Romaeus Leuven, OCD. Translated by Hilda Graef. Chicago: Henry Regnery Company, 1960.

Stewart, Columba. *Cassian the Monk*. Oxford Studies in Historical Theology. New York: Oxford University Press, 1998.

Strathern, Paul. *Heidegger in 90 Minutes*. Chicago: Ivan R. Dee, 2002.

Straw, Carole. *Gregory the Great: Perfection in Imperfection*. Berkeley: University of California Press, 1988.

Tarnas, Richard. *The Passion of the Western Mind: Understanding the Ideas That Have Shaped Our World View*. New York: Ballantine Books, 1991.

Taylor, Charles. *Sources of the Self: The Making of the Modern Identity*. Cambridge, MA: Harvard University Press, 1989.

Teresa of Ávila. *The Collected Works of St. Teresa of Ávila*. Vol. 1, *The Book of Her Life, Spiritual Testimonies, Soliloquies*. Translated by Kieran Kavanaugh, OCD, and Otilio Rodriguez, OCD. Washington, DC: Institute of Carmelite Studies, 1976.

———. *The Interior Castle*. Translated and edited by E. Allison Peers. Garden City, NY: Doubleday, 1961.

Thérèse of Lisieux. *Story of a Soul: The Autobiography of St. Thérèse of Lisieux*. Translated by John Clarke, OCD. 3rd ed. Washington, DC: Institute of Carmelite Studies, 1996.

Underhill, Evelyn. *Mysticism: The Nature and Development of Spiritual Consciousness*. Oxford: Oneworld Publications, 1993.

Vauchez, André. *The Spirituality of the Medieval West: The Eighth to the Twelfth Century*. Translated by Colette Friedlander. Cistercian Studies 145. Kalamazoo, MI: Cistercian Publications, 1993.

Vogüé, Adalbert de, OSB. "The Greater Rules of St. Basil—A Survey." In *In Honor of St. Basil the Great*. Word and Spirit 1. Still River, MA: St. Bede's Publications, 1979.

——. *The Rule of Saint Benedict: A Doctrinal and Spiritual Commentary*. Translated by John Baptist Hasbrouck. Kalamazoo, MI: Cistercian Publications, 1983.

Wallace, Susan Helen, FSP. *Saint Thérèse of Lisieux: With Confidence and Love*. Boston: Pauline Books and Media, 1998.

Weisheipl, James A., OP. *Friar Thomas D'Aquino: His Life, Thought, and Work*. Garden City, NY: Doubleday, 1974.

Wilkie, Brian, and James Hurt, comps. *Literature of the Western World*. Vol. 1, *The Ancient World through the Renaissance*. 4th ed. Upper Saddle River, NJ: Prentice Hall, 1992.

——. *Literature of the Western World*. Vol. 2, *Neoclassicism through the Modern Period*. 4th ed. Upper Saddle River, NJ: Prentice Hall, 1992.

Also by Paula Huston

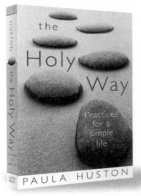

$15.95 Pb

The Holy Way:
Practices for a Simple Life

Drawing on the powerful histories of the saints and her personal experience as a professor, wife, and mother, Huston offers practical guidance to pursuing and achieving spiritual simplicity in a chaotic world. In *The Holy Way*, she examines a variety of spiritual practices in the Christian tradition that lead to a simpler life and tells stories of faith that exemplify the transformative power of being alone with God.

The Holy Way:
Discussion Guide

This guide provides material for one book group orientation and five discussion sessions. Each session is based on a theme and includes a short prayer, group discussion questions, and questions for individual reflection. Use this guide to enrich your reading of *The Holy Way*.

$9.95 Pb

Available through your local bookstore or by ordering direct

LOYOLAPRESS. www.loyolabooks.org ◆ 800-621-1008

A SPECIAL INVITATION

Loyola Press invites you to become one of our Loyola Press Advisors! Join our unique online community of people willing to share with us their thoughts and ideas about Catholic life and faith. By sharing your perspective, you will help us improve our books and serve the greater Catholic community.

From time to time, registered advisors are invited to participate in online surveys and discussion groups. Most surveys will take less than ten minutes to complete. Loyola Press will recognize your time and efforts with gift certificates and prizes. Your personal information will be held in strict confidence. Your participation will be for research purposes only, and at no time will we try to sell you anything.

Please consider this opportunity to help Loyola Press improve our products and better serve you and the Catholic community. To learn more or to join, visit **www.SpiritedTalk.org** and register today.

—The Loyola Press Advisory Team